Mike Holt's Illustrated Guide to

Understanding NEC® Requirements for
LIMITED ENERGY &
COMMUNICATIONS SYSTEMS

Based on the 2014 NEC®

Mike Holt Enterprises, Inc.
888.NEC.CODE (632.2633) • www.MikeHolt.com

NOTICE TO THE READER

Mike Holt's Illustrated Guide to Understanding NEC® Requirements for Limited Energy & Communications Systems, based on the 2014 NEC®

First Printing: July 2014

Author: Mike Holt
Technical Illustrator: Mike Culbreath
Cover Design: Madalina Iordache-Levay
Layout Design and Typesetting: Cathleen Kwas

COPYRIGHT © 2014 Charles Michael Holt
ISBN 978-1-932685-73-2

Produced and Printed in the USA

This logo is a registered trademark of Mike Holt Enterprises, Inc.

If you are an instructor and would like to request an examination copy of this or other Mike Holt Publications:

Call: 888.NEC.CODE (632.2633) • Fax: 352.360.0983
E-mail: Info@MikeHolt.com • Visit: www.MikeHolt.com

You can download a sample PDF of all our publications by visiting www.MikeHolt.com

I dedicate this book to the
Lord Jesus Christ, my mentor and teacher

Our Commitment

We are committed to serving the electrical industry with integrity and respect by always searching for the most accurate interpretation of the NEC® and creating the highest quality instructional material that makes learning easy.

We are invested in the idea of changing lives, and build our products with the goal of not only helping you meet your licensing requirements, but also with the goal that this knowledge will improve your expertise in the field and help you throughout your career.

We are committed to building a life-long relationship with you, and to helping you in each stage of your electrical career. Whether you are an apprentice just getting started in the industry, or an electrician preparing to take an exam, we are here to help you. When you need Continuing Education credits to renew your license, we will do everything we can to get our online courses and seminars approved in your state. Or if you are a contractor looking to train your team, we have a solution for you. And if you have advanced to the point where you are now teaching others, we are here to help you build your program and provide tools to make that task easier.

We genuinely care about providing quality electrical training that will help you take your skills to the next level.

Thanks for choosing Mike Holt Enterprises for your electrical training needs. We are here to help you every step of the way and encourage you to contact us so we can be a part of your success.

God bless,

TABLE OF CONTENTS

ABOUT THIS TEXTBOOK

Mike Holt's Illustrated Guide to Understanding NEC® Requirements for Limited Energy & Communications Systems

This edition of *Mike Holt's Illustrated Guide to Understanding NEC® Requirements for Limited Energy & Communications Systems* is intended to provide you with the tools necessary to understand the technical requirements of the *National Electrical Code® (NEC)* in regard to limited energy and communications systems.

The writing style of this textbook is meant to be informative, practical, useful, easy to read, and applicable for everyday use. Just like all of Mike Holt's textbooks, this one contains hundreds of full-color illustrations showing the safety requirements of the *National Electrical Code* in practical use, helping you visualize the *Code* in today's electrical installations.

This illustrated textbook contains cautions regarding possible conflicts or confusing *NEC* requirements, tips on proper electrical installations, and warnings of dangers related to improper electrical installations. In spite of this effort, some rules may still seem unclear or need additional editorial improvement.

We can't eliminate confusing, conflicting, or controversial *Code* requirements, but we do try to put them into sharper focus to help you understand their intended purpose. Sometimes a requirement is confusing and it might be hard to understand its actual application. When this occurs, this textbook will point the situation out in an upfront and straightforward manner. We apologize in advance if that ever seems disrespectful, but our intention is to help the industry understand the current *NEC* as best as possible, point out areas that need refinement, and encourage *Code* users to be a part of the change process that creates a better *NEC* for the future.

The Scope of this Textbook

This textbook covers the requirements for wiring for control, signal and communications systems that Mike considers to be of critical importance in Articles 90, 300, 725, 760, 770, 800, 810 and 820.

This textbook is written with these stipulations:

1. **Power Systems and Voltage.** All power-supply systems are assumed to be one of the following, unless identified otherwise:

   - 2-wire, single-phase, 120V
   - 3-wire, single-phase, 120/240V
   - 4-wire, three-phase, 120/240V Delta
   - 4-wire, three-phase, 120/208V or 277/480V Wye

2. **Electrical Calculations.** Unless the questions or examples specify three-phase, they're based on a single-phase power supply. In addition, all amperage calculations are rounded to the nearest ampere in accordance with Section 220.5(B).

3. **Conductor Material.** Conductors are assumed to be copper, unless aluminum is identified or specified.

4. **Conductor Sizing.** Conductors are sized based on a THHN/THWN-2 copper conductor terminating on a 75°C terminal in accordance with 110.14(C), unless the question or example indicates otherwise.

5. **Overcurrent Device.** The term "overcurrent device" refers to a molded-case circuit breaker, unless specified otherwise. Where a fuse is specified, it's a single-element type fuse, also known as a "one-time fuse," unless the text specifies otherwise.

This textbook is to be used along with the *NEC*, not as a replacement for it. Be sure to have a copy of the 2014 *National Electrical Code* handy. Compare what's being explained in this textbook to what the *Code* book says, and discuss with others any topics that you find difficult to understand.

You'll notice that we've paraphrased a great deal of the *NEC* wording, and some of the article and section titles appear different from the text in the actual *Code* book. We believe doing so makes it easier to understand the content of the rule, so keep this in mind when comparing this textbook to the actual *NEC*.

This textbook follows the *NEC* format, but it doesn't cover every *Code* requirement. For example, it doesn't include every article, section, subsection, exception, or Informational Note. So don't be concerned if you see that the textbook contains Exception 1 and Exception 3, but not Exception 2.

We hope that as you read through this textbook, you'll allow sufficient time to review the text along with the outstanding graphics and examples, which are invaluable to your understanding.

How to Use This Textbook

The layout of this textbook incorporates special features designed not only to help you navigate easily through the material but to enhance your understanding as well.

■ **Bulleted Author's Comments** are intended to help you understand the *NEC* material and background information.

2014 CC **Graphics with an icon and green border** contain a 2014 *Code* change, with *NEC* text changes underlined in green. Green-bordered graphics with no green underlined text most likely indicate that the change is the removal of some text. Graphics without a colored border support the concept being discussed, and nothing in the graphic was affected by a change for 2014.

A QR code in the corresponding text can be scanned with a smartphone app to take you to a sample video clip so you can watch Mike and the DVD panel discuss this topic.

Text that's underlined in the chapter color denotes a change in the *Code* for 2014.

Framed white notes contain examples and practical application questions and answers.

Color coding and a modular format make it easy to navigate through each section of the textbook.

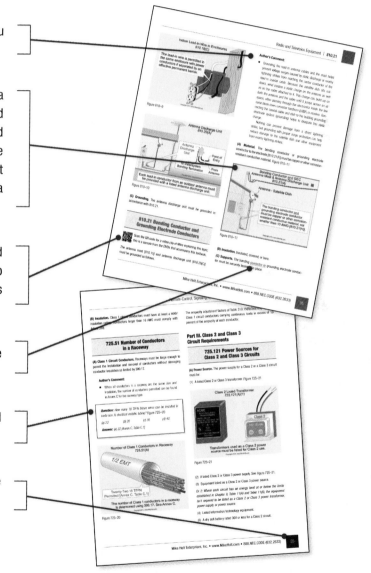

Cross-References, Notes, and Exceptions

Cross-References. This textbook contains several *NEC* cross-references to other related *Code* requirements to help you develop a better understanding of how the *NEC* rules relate to one another. These cross-references are indicated by *Code* section numbers in brackets, an example of which is "[90.4]."

Informational Notes. Informational Notes contained in the *NEC* will be identified in this textbook as "Note."

Exceptions. Exceptions contained in this textbook will be identified as "Ex" and not spelled out.

Textbook Corrections

We're committed to providing you the finest product with the fewest errors. We take great care in proofreading and researching the *NEC* requirements to ensure this textbook is correct, but we're realistic and know that there may be errors found and reported after this textbook is printed. This can occur because the *NEC* is dramatically changed each *Code* cycle; new articles are added, some are deleted, some are relocated, and many are renumbered.

The last thing we want is for you to have problems finding, communicating, or accessing this information. Any errors found after printing are listed on our website, so if you find an error, first check to see if it's already been corrected by going to www.MikeHolt.com, click on "Books," and then click on "Corrections" (www.MikeHolt.com/book-corrections.htm).

If you believe that there's an error of any kind (typographical, grammatical, technical, or anything else) in this textbook or in the Answer Key and it isn't already listed on the website, e-mail Corrections@MikeHolt.com. Be sure to include the textbook title, page number, and any other pertinent information.

If you have adopted Mike Holt textbooks for use in your classroom you can register for up-to-date Answer Keys that can be downloaded from our website. To register and receive a log-in password, go to our web site www.MikeHolt.com, click on "Instructors" in the sidebar of links, and then click on "Answer Keys." On this same page you'll also find instructions for accessing and downloading these Answer Keys. Please note that this feature will only work after you've received a log-in password.

Technical Questions

As you progress through this textbook, you might find that you don't understand every explanation, example, calculation, or comment. Don't become frustrated, and don't get down on yourself. Remember, this is the *National Electrical Code*, and sometimes the best attempt to explain a concept isn't enough to make it perfectly clear. If you're still confused, visit www.MikeHolt.com, and post your question on our free Code Forum for help. The forum is a moderated community of electrical professionals where you can exchange ideas and post technical questions that will be answered by your peers.

QR Codes

What's this symbol? It's a QR code and gives you the ability to use your smartphone to scan the image (using a barcode reader app) and be directed to a website. For example, the QR code to the right (when captured) will direct your smartphone to the Mike Holt Enterprises website. We've included these in various places in our textbook to make it easier for you to go directly to the website page referenced.

Follow the QR Code! When you see a QR code next to a section in the text, scan it with your smartphone to bring it to life. You will be able to watch a video clip that shows Mike and his panel of experts discussing this topic.

These video clips are samples from the DVD that was created for this book. Whether you're a visual or an auditory learner, watching this DVD will enhance your knowledge and understanding as you read through the textbook.

To order the DVD that accompanies this textbook at a discounted price, call our office at 888.632.2633.

Additional Products to Help You Learn

Understanding 2014 NEC Requirements for Limited Energy & Communications Systems DVD

One of the best ways to get the most out of this textbook is to use it in conjunction with the corresponding DVD. Mike Holt's DVD provides a 360° view of each topic with specialized commentary from Mike Holt and his panel of industry experts. Whether you're a visual or an auditory learner, watching the DVD will enhance your knowledge and understanding.

To order a copy of the DVD at a discounted price, call our office at 888.632.2633.

Electrical Theory DVD Library

Only when you truly know electrical theory can you have confidence in the practical aspects of your electrical work. The topics in Mike's Electrical Theory Library will help you understand what electricity is, how it's produced and how it's used. You'll learn to perform basic electrical calculations necessary for everyday use. The crucial study of circuits will help you understand complicated circuits for controls, fire alarms, security and much more. In addition, the basics for understanding motors and transformers are clearly explained. The most important subject you will learn about is grounding!

This program includes the *Basic Electrical Theory* textbook and the following DVDs:

- Electrical Fundamentals and Basic Electricity
- Electrical Circuits, Systems and Protection
- Alternating Current, Motors, Generators, and Transformers

To order, visit www.MikeHolt.com/Theory, scan this QR code, or call 888.632.2633.

Detailed *Code* Library

When you really need to understand the *NEC*, there's no better way to learn it than with Mike's Detailed *Code* Library. It takes you step-by-step through the *NEC*, in *Code* order with detailed illustrations, great practice questions, and in-depth DVD analysis. This library is perfect for engineers, electricians, contractors, and electrical inspectors.

- *Understanding the National Electrical Code—Volume 1*
- *Understanding the National Electrical Code—Volume 2*
- *NEC Exam Practice Questions* workbook
- General Requirements DVD
- Wiring and Protection DVD
- Grounding versus Bonding DVDs (2)
- Wiring Methods and Materials DVDs (2)
- Equipment for General Use DVD
- Special Occupancies DVD
- Special Equipment DVD
- Limited Energy and Communications Systems DVD

To order, visit www.MikeHolt.com/14DECO, scan this QR code, or call 888.632.2633.

2014 *Code* Book and Tabs

Whether you prefer the softbound, spiral bound, or the loose-leaf version, everyone should have an updated *Code* book for accurate reference. Placing tabs on *Code* articles, sections, and tables will make it easier for you to use the *NEC*. However, too many tabs will defeat the purpose. Mike's best-selling tabs make organizing your *Code* book easy.

To order your *Code* book and set of tabs, visit www.MikeHolt.com/14Code or call 1.888.NEC.CODE (632.2633).

ABOUT THE
NATIONAL ELECTRICAL CODE

The *National Electrical Code* is written for persons who understand electrical terms, theory, safety procedures, and electrical trade practices. These individuals include electricians, electrical contractors, electrical inspectors, electrical engineers, designers, and other qualified persons. The *Code* isn't written to serve as an instructional or teaching manual for untrained individuals [90.1(A)].

Learning to use the *NEC* can be likened to learning the strategy needed to play the game of chess well; it's a great game if you enjoy mental warfare. When learning to play chess, you must first learn the names of the game pieces, how they're placed on the board, and how each one is moved.

Once you understand the fundamentals, you're ready to start playing the game. Unfortunately, at this point all you can do is make crude moves, because you really don't understand how all the information works together. To play chess well, you'll need to learn how to use your knowledge by working on subtle strategies before you can work your way up to the more intriguing and complicated moves.

The *Code* is updated every three years to accommodate new electrical products and materials, changing technologies, improved installation techniques, and to make editorial refinements to improve readability and application. While the uniform adoption of each new edition of the *NEC* is the best approach for all involved in the electrical industry, many inspection jurisdictions modify the *Code* when it's adopted. To further complicate this situation, the *NEC* allows the authority having jurisdiction, typically the "Electrical Inspector," the flexibility to waive specific *Code* requirements, and to permit alternative methods. This is only allowed when he or she is assured the completed electrical installation is equivalent in establishing and maintaining effective safety [90.4].

Keeping up with requirements of the *Code* should be the goal of everyone involved in the safety of electrical installations. This includes electrical installers, contractors, owners, inspectors, engineers, instructors, and others concerned with electrical installations.

About the 2014 *NEC*

The actual process of changing the *Code* takes about two years, and it involves hundreds of individuals making an effort to have the *NEC* as current and accurate as possible. Let's review how this process worked for the 2014 *NEC*:

Step 1. Proposals—November, 2011. Anybody can submit a proposal to change the *Code* before the proposal closing date. Thousands of proposals were submitted to modify the 2011 *NEC* and create the 2014 *Code*. Of these proposals, several hundred rules were revised that significantly affect the electrical industry. Some changes were editorial revisions, while others were more significant, such as new articles, sections, exceptions, and Informational Notes.

Step 2. *Code*-Making Panel(s) Review Proposals—January, 2012. All *Code* change proposals were reviewed by *Code*-Making Panels. There were 19 panels in the 2014 revision process who voted to accept, reject, or modify proposals.

Step 3. Report on Proposals (ROP)—July, 2012. The voting of the *Code*-Making Panels on the proposals was published for public review in a document called the "Report on Proposals," frequently referred to as the "ROP."

Step 4. Public Comments—October, 2012. Once the ROP was available, public comments were submitted asking the *Code*-Making Panel members to revise their earlier actions on change proposals, based on new information. The closing date for "Comments" was October, 2012.

Step 5. Comments Reviewed by *Code* Panels—December, 2012. The *Code*-Making Panels met again to review, discuss, and vote on public comments.

Step 6. Report on Comments (ROC)—March, 2013. The voting on the "Comments" was published for public review in a document called the "Report on Comments," frequently referred to as the "ROC."

Step 7. Electrical Section—June, 2013. The NFPA Electrical Section discussed and reviewed the work of the *Code*-Making Panels. The Electrical Section developed recommendations on last-minute motions to revise the proposed *NEC* draft that would be presented at the NFPA's annual meeting.

Step 8. NFPA Annual Meeting—June, 2013. The 2014 *NEC* was voted by the NFPA members to approve the action of the *Code*-Making Panels at the annual meeting, after a number of motions (often called "floor actions" or "NITMAMs") were voted on.

Step 9. Standards Council Review Appeals and Approves the 2014 *NEC*—July, 2013. The NFPA Standards Council reviewed the record of the *Code*-making process and approved publication of the 2014 *NEC*.

Step 10. 2014 *NEC* Published—September, 2013. The 2014 *National Electrical Code* was published, following the NFPA Board of Directors review of appeals.

Author's Comment:

■ Proposals and comments can be submitted online at the NFPA website (www.nfpa.org). From the homepage, click on "Codes and Standards", then find NFPA 70 (*National Electrical Code*). From there, follow the on screen instructions to download the proposal form. The deadline for proposals to create the 2017 *National Electrical Code* will be around November of 2014. If you would like to see something changed in the *Code*, you're encouraged to participate in the process.

Not a Game

Electrical work isn't a game, and it must be taken very seriously. Learning the basics of electricity, important terms and concepts, as well as the basic layout of the *NEC* gives you just enough knowledge to be dangerous. There are thousands of specific and unique applications of electrical installations, and the *Code* doesn't cover every one of them. To safely apply the *NEC*, you must understand the purpose of a rule and how it affects the safety aspects of the installation.

NEC Terms and Concepts

The *NEC* contains many technical terms, so it's crucial for *Code* users to understand their meanings and their applications. If you don't understand a term used in a *Code* rule, it will be impossible to properly apply the *NEC* requirement. Be sure you understand that Article 100 defines the terms that apply to two or more *Code* articles. For example, the term "Dwelling Unit" is found in many articles; if you don't know what a dwelling unit is, how can you apply the requirements for it?

In addition, many articles have terms unique for that specific article and definitions of those terms are only applicable for that given article. For example, Section 250.2 contains the definitions of terms that only apply to Article 250—Grounding and Bonding.

Small Words, Grammar, and Punctuation

It's not only the technical words that require close attention, because even the simplest of words can make a big difference to the application of a rule. The word "or" can imply alternate choices for wiring methods, while "and" can mean an additional requirement. Let's not forget about grammar and punctuation. The location of a comma can dramatically change the requirement of a rule.

Slang Terms or Technical Jargon

Electricians, engineers, and other trade-related professionals use slang terms or technical jargon that isn't shared by all. This makes it very difficult to communicate because not everybody understands the intent or application of those slang terms. So where possible, be sure you use the proper word, and don't use a word if you don't understand its definition and application. For example, lots of electricians use the term "pigtail" when describing the short conductor for the connection of a receptacle, switch, luminaire, or equipment. Although they may understand it, not everyone does.

NEC Style and Layout

Before we get into the details of the *NEC*, we need to take a few moments to understand its style and layout. Understanding the structure and writing style of the *Code* is very important before it can be used and applied effectively. The *National Electrical Code* is organized into ten major components.

1. Table of Contents
2. Article 90 (Introduction to the *Code*)
3. Chapters 1 through 9 (major categories)
4. Articles 90 through 840 (individual subjects)
5. Parts (divisions of an article)
6. Sections and Tables (*NEC* requirements)
7. Exceptions (*Code* permissions)
8. Informational Notes (explanatory material)
9. Annexes (information)
10. Index

1. Table of Contents. The Table of Contents displays the layout of the chapters, articles, and parts as well as the page numbers. It's an excellent resource and should be referred to periodically to observe the interrelationship of the various *NEC* components. When attempting to locate the rules for a particular situation, knowledgeable *Code* users often go first to the Table of Contents to quickly find the specific *NEC* Part that applies.

2. Introduction. The *NEC* begins with Article 90, the introduction to the *Code*. It contains the purpose of the *NEC*, what's covered and what isn't covered along with how the *Code* is arranged. It also gives information on enforcement and how mandatory and permissive rules are written as well as how explanatory material is included. Article 90 also includes information on formal interpretations, examination of equipment for safety, wiring planning, and information about formatting units of measurement.

3. Chapters. There are nine chapters, each of which is divided into articles. The articles fall into one of four groupings: General Requirements (Chapters 1 through 4), Specific Requirements (Chapters 5 through 7), Communications Systems (Chapter 8), and Tables (Chapter 9).

Chapter 1—General
Chapter 2—Wiring and Protection
Chapter 3—Wiring Methods and Materials
Chapter 4—Equipment for General Use
Chapter 5—Special Occupancies
Chapter 6—Special Equipment
Chapter 7—Special Conditions
Chapter 8—Communications Systems (Telephone, Data, Satellite, Cable TV and Broadband)
Chapter 9—Tables–Conductor and Raceway Specifications

4. Articles. The *NEC* contains approximately 140 articles, each of which covers a specific subject. For example:

Article 110—General Requirements
Article 250—Grounding and Bonding
Article 300—General Requirements for Wiring Methods and Materials
Article 430—Motors and Motor Controllers
Article 500—Hazardous (Classified) Locations
Article 680—Swimming Pools, Fountains, and Similar Installations
Article 725—Remote-Control, Signaling, and Power-Limited Circuits
Article 800—Communications Circuits

5. Parts. Larger articles are subdivided into parts. Because the parts of a *Code* article aren't included in the section numbers, we have a tendency to forget what "part" the *NEC* rule is relating to. For example, Table 110.34(A) contains working space clearances for electrical equipment. If we aren't careful, we might think this table applies to all electrical installations, but Table 110.34(A) is located in Part III, which only contains requirements for "Over 600 Volts, Nominal" installations. The rules for working clearances for electrical equipment for systems 600V, nominal, or less are contained in Table 110.26(A)(1), which is located in Part II—600 Volts, Nominal, or Less.

6. Sections and Tables.

Sections. Each *NEC* rule is called a "*Code* Section." A *Code* section may be broken down into subsections by letters in parentheses (A), (B), and so on. Numbers in parentheses (1), (2), and so forth, may further break down a subsection, and lowercase letters (a), (b), and so on, further break the rule down to the third level. For example, the rule requiring all receptacles in a dwelling unit bathroom to be GFCI protected is contained in Section 210.8(A)(1). Section 210.8(A)(1) is located in Chapter 2, Article 210, Section 8, Subsection (A), Sub-subsection (1).

Many in the industry incorrectly use the term "Article" when referring to a *Code* section. For example, they say "Article 210.8," when they should say "Section 210.8." Section numbers in this textbook are shown without the word "Section," unless they begin a sentence. For example, Section 210.8(A) is shown as simply 210.8(A).

Tables. Many *NEC* requirements are contained within tables, which are lists of *Code* rules placed in a systematic arrangement. The titles of the tables are extremely important; you must read them carefully in order to understand the contents, applications, limitations, and so forth, of each table in the *NEC*. Many times notes are provided in or below a table; be sure to read them as well since they're also part of the requirement. For example, Note 1 for Table 300.5 explains how to measure the cover when burying cables and raceways, and Note 5 explains what to do if solid rock is encountered.

7. Exceptions. Exceptions are *Code* requirements or permissions that provide an alternative method to a specific rule. There are two types of exceptions—mandatory and permissive. When a rule has several exceptions, those exceptions with mandatory requirements are listed before the permissive exceptions.

Mandatory Exceptions. A mandatory exception uses the words "shall" or "shall not." The word "shall" in an exception means that if you're using the exception, you're required to do it in a particular way. The phrase "shall not" means it isn't permitted.

Permissive Exceptions. A permissive exception uses words such as "shall be permitted," which means it's acceptable (but not mandatory) to do it in this way.

8. Informational Notes. An Informational Note contains explanatory material intended to clarify a rule or give assistance, but it isn't a *Code* requirement.

9. Annexes. Annexes aren't a part of the *NEC* requirements, and are included in the *Code* for informational purposes only.

Annex A. Product Safety Standards

Annex B. Application Information for Ampacity Calculation

Annex C. Raceway Fill Tables for Conductors and Fixture Wires of the Same Size

Annex D. Examples

Annex E. Types of Construction

Annex F. Critical Operations Power Systems (COPS)

Annex G. Supervisory Control and Data Acquisition (SCADA)

Annex H. Administration and Enforcement

Annex I. Recommended Tightening Torques

Annex J. ADA Standards for Accessible Design

10. Index. The Index at the back of the *Code* book is helpful in locating a specific rule.

Changes to the *NEC* since the previous edition(s), are identified by shading, but rules that have been relocated aren't identified as a change. A bullet symbol "•" is located on the margin to indicate the location of a rule that was deleted from a previous edition. New articles contain a vertical line in the margin of the page.

Different Interpretations

Some electricians, contractors, instructors, inspectors, engineers, and others enjoy the challenge of discussing the *NEC* requirements, hopefully in a positive and productive manner. This give-and-take is important to the process of better understanding the *Code* requirements and application(s). However, if you're going to participate in an *NEC* discussion, please don't spout out what you think without having the actual *Code* book in your hand. The professional way of discussing an *NEC* requirement is by referring to a specific section, rather than talking in vague generalities.

How to Locate a Specific Requirement

How to go about finding what you're looking for in the *Code* book depends, to some degree, on your experience with the *NEC*. *Code* experts typically know the requirements so well they just go to the correct rule without any outside assistance. The Table of Contents might be the only thing very experienced *NEC* users need to locate the requirement they're looking for. On the other hand, average *Code* users should use all of the tools at their disposal, including the Table of Contents and the Index.

Table of Contents. Let's work out a simple example: What *NEC* rule specifies the maximum number of disconnects permitted for a service? If you're an experienced *Code* user, you'll know Article 230 applies to "Services," and because this article is so large, it's divided up into multiple parts (actually eight parts). With this knowledge, you can quickly go to the Table of Contents and see it lists the Service Equipment Disconnecting Means requirements in Part VI.

Author's Comment:

■ The number 70 precedes all page numbers because the *NEC* is NFPA Standard Number 70.

Index. If you use the Index, which lists subjects in alphabetical order, to look up the term "service disconnect," you'll see there's no listing. If you try "disconnecting means," then "services," you'll find that the Index indicates that the rule is located in Article 230, Part VI. Because the *NEC* doesn't give a page number in the Index, you'll need to use the Table of Contents to find it, or flip through the *Code* book to Article 230, then continue to flip through pages until you find Part VI.

Many people complain that the *NEC* only confuses them by taking them in circles. As you gain experience in using the *Code* and deepen your understanding of words, terms, principles, and practices, you'll find the *NEC* much easier to understand and use than you originally thought.

Customizing Your *Code* Book

One way to increase your comfort level with the *Code* book is to customize it to meet your needs. You can do this by highlighting and underlining important *NEC* requirements, and by attaching tabs to important pages. Be aware that if you're using your *Code* book to take an exam, some exam centers don't allow markings of any type.

Highlighting. As you read through this textbook, be sure you highlight those requirements in the *Code* that are the most important or relevant to you. Use one color for general interest and a different one for important requirements you want to find quickly. Be sure to highlight terms in the Index and the Table of Contents as you use them.

Underlining. Underline or circle key words and phrases in the *NEC* with a red pen (not a lead pencil) and use a short ruler or other straightedge to keep lines straight and neat. This is a very handy way to make important requirements stand out. A short ruler or other straightedge also comes in handy for locating specific information in the many *Code* tables.

ABOUT THE AUTHOR

Mike Holt—Author

Founder and President
Mike Holt Enterprises
Groveland, FL
www.MikeHolt.com

Mike Holt worked his way up through the electrical trade. He began as an apprentice electrician and became one of the most recognized experts in the world as it relates to electrical power installations. He's worked as a journeyman electrician, master electrician, and electrical contractor. Mike's experience in the real world gives him a unique understanding of how the *NEC* relates to electrical installations from a practical standpoint. You'll find his writing style to be direct, nontechnical, and powerful.

Did you know Mike didn't finish high school? So if you struggled in high school or didn't finish at all, don't let it get you down. However, realizing that success depends on one's continuing pursuit of education, Mike immediately attained his GED, and ultimately attended the University of Miami's Graduate School for a Master's degree in Business Administration.

Mike resides in Central Florida, is the father of seven children, has five grandchildren, and enjoys many outside interests and activities. He's a nine-time National Barefoot Water-Ski Champion (1988, 1999, 2005–2009, 2012–2013). He's set many national records and continues to train year-round at a World competition level (www.barefootwaterskier.com).

What sets him apart from some is his commitment to living a balanced lifestyle; placing God first, family, career, then self.

Special Acknowledgments—First, I want to thank God for my godly wife who's always by my side and my children, Belynda, Melissa, Autumn, Steven, Michael, Meghan, and Brittney.

A special thank you must be sent to the staff at the National Fire Protection Association (NFPA), publishers of the *NEC*—in particular Jeff Sargent for his assistance in answering my many *Code* questions over the years. Jeff, you're a "first class" guy, and I admire your dedication and commitment to helping others understand the *NEC*. Other former NFPA staff members I would like to thank include John Caloggero, Joe Ross, and Dick Murray for their help in the past.

A personal thank you goes to Sarina, my long-time friend and office manager. It's been wonderful working side-by-side with you for over 25 years nurturing this company's growth from its small beginnings.

Mike Holt's Understanding 2014 NEC Requirements for Limited Energy & Communications Systems

ABOUT THE ILLUSTRATOR

Mike Culbreath—Illustrator

Graphic Illustrator
Alden, MI
www.MikeHolt.com

Mike Culbreath devoted his career to the electrical industry and worked his way up from an apprentice electrician to master electrician. He started in the electrical field doing residential and light commercial construction. He later did service work and custom electrical installations. While working as a journeyman electrician, he suffered a serious on-the-job knee injury. As part of his rehabilitation, Mike completed courses at Mike Holt Enterprises, and then passed the exam to receive his Master Electrician's license. In 1986, with a keen interest in continuing education for electricians, he joined the staff to update material and began illustrating Mike Holt's textbooks and magazine articles.

He started with simple hand-drawn diagrams and cut-and-paste graphics. When frustrated by the limitations of that style of illustrating, he took a company computer home to learn how to operate some basic computer graphic software. Becoming aware that computer graphics offered a lot of flexibility for creating illustrations, Mike took every computer graphics class and seminar he could to help develop his computer graphic skills. He's now worked as an illustrator and editor with the company for over 25 years and, as Mike Holt has proudly acknowledged, has helped to transform his words and visions into lifelike graphics.

Originally from South Florida, Mike now lives in northern lower Michigan where he enjoys kayaking, photography, and cooking, but his real passion is his horses.

Mike loves spending time with his children Dawn and Mac and his grandchildren Jonah and Kieley.

Special Acknowledgments—I would like to thank Ryan Jackson, an outstanding and very knowledgeable *Code* guy, and Eric Stromberg, an electrical engineer and super geek (and I mean that in the most complimentary manner, this guy is brilliant), for helping me keep our graphics as technically correct as possible.

I also want to give a special thank you to Cathleen Kwas for making me look good with her outstanding layout design and typesetting skills and Toni Culbreath who proofreads all of my material. I would also like to acknowledge Belynda Holt Pinto, our Chief Operations Officer and the rest of the outstanding staff at Mike Holt Enterprises, for all the hard work they do to help produce and distribute these outstanding products.

And last but not least, I need to give a special thank you to Mike Holt for not firing me over 25 years ago when I "borrowed" one of his computers and took it home to begin the process of learning how to do computer illustrations. He gave me the opportunity and time needed to develop my computer graphic skills. He's been an amazing friend and mentor since I met him as a student many years ago. Thanks for believing in me and allowing me to be part of the Mike Holt Enterprises family.

ABOUT THE TEAM

Editorial and Production Team

A special thanks goes to **Toni Culbreath** for her outstanding contribution to this project. She worked tirelessly to proofread and edit this publication. Her attention to detail and dedication is irreplaceable.

Many thanks to **Cathleen Kwas** who n, layout, and production of this book. Her desire to create the best possible product for our customers is greatly appreciated.

Also, thanks to **Paula Birchfield** who was the Production Coordinator of the textbook. She helped keep everything flowing and tied up all the loose ends.

Thanks to **Bruce Marcho** for doing such an excellent job recording, editing, and producing our DVDs. Bruce has played a vital role in the production of our products for over 25 years.

Video Team

John Paul David

Director of Corporate Safety and Training
Staley, Inc.
Little Rock, AR
www.staleyinc.com

John Paul David is responsible for training all Staley, Inc. employees on the industry's safety policies and standards. Additionally, he's the in-house instructor for Staley's BICSI certified training center which is utilized company-wide by technicians. John also oversees the maintenance of facilities at the headquarters in Little Rock, Arkansas.

John is a Master Electrician in multiple jurisdictions and is a certified trainer and Level 3 BICSI Technician in design, integration, installation, and infrastructure in the telecommunications industry. BICSI is a professional association that provides technical education, information,

and knowledge assessment for the information and communications technology (ICT) community.

John began his career with Staley, Inc. as an Electrical Apprentice. After completing a four-year BAT Electrical Apprenticeship program, he went on to earn his Journeyman and Master licenses as well as his BICSI certifications.

He resides in Little Rock with his wife. Together, they have a beautiful daughter, age 8, and son, age 5. John is an active member of his church where he works with the children's group in a leadership position.

Daniel Brian House

Dan House Electric, Inc.
Ocala, FL
www.DanHouseElectric.com

Brian House is a high-energy entrepreneur with a passion for doing business the right way. Brian is currently the CEO of Dan House Electric, Inc., an unlimited electrical contracting company based in Florida and working throughout the southeast United States.

Brian has been involved in varying aspects of electrical contracting and energy conservation since the 1990s. He has a passion for constantly improving the combinations of technology offered to his customers, whether it is designing energy-efficient lighting retrofits, exploring "green" biomass generators, or partnering with solar energy companies as their preferred installer. Brian has experienced the ups and downs of electrical contracting and enjoys the challenges of design build projects.

Passionate about helping others, he regularly engages with the youth of the local community to motivate them into exploring their future.

Brian and his wife Carissa have shared the joy of their four children and over 30 foster children during a happy 16 years of marriage. When not at work or church, he can be found racing mountain bikes with his kids or on the action-packed intercoastals as an avid fly fisherman.

Ryan Jackson

Electrical Inspector
Draper City, UT

Ryan Jackson is an electrical consultant in the Salt Lake City, Utah, area who began his career as a carpenter while in high school. He began doing electrical work when he was 18 and, at the age of 23, Ryan landed his first job as an electrical inspector and subsequently became certified in building, plumbing, and mechanical inspection (commercial and residential), as well as building and electrical plan review. Two years after becoming an inspector, he was approached by a friend in the area asking him to fill in for him at an electrical seminar. After his first class Ryan was hooked, and is now a highly sought after seminar instructor. He's taught in several states, and loves helping people increase their understanding of the *Code*.

Ryan met Mike in 2005 and helped with his 2005 *Understanding the NEC, Volume 2* videos and textbooks. He believes there are only a few opportunities that can change a person's life and career—and meeting Mike was one of them.

When Ryan isn't working, he can often be found in his garage turning wood on his lathe, or in the kitchen where he enjoys wine making. Ryan married his high school sweetheart, Sharie, and they have two beautiful children together: Kaitlynn and Aaron.

George Stolz

Master Electrician
Quicksilver Electrical Training
Pierce, CO
www.qstrain.com

George Stolz began his electrical career by tinkering around with machines in the Production Department of the Fort Collins *Coloradoan*. He began his apprenticeship in 2002 and developed a keen interest in the *Code* shortly after joining the trade. George currently serves as a construction foreman for Gregory Electric in Loveland, Colorado. His work experience includes single- and multi-family dwellings, hospitals, schools, grocery stores, aircraft hangars, office buildings, maintenance, estimating, and project management.

George is a moderator on Mike Holt's Internet *Code* Forum, which he asserts is the best place to go for technical discussion on the web. He also teaches classes at the Independent Electrical Contractors Rocky Mountain Chapter.

George lives near Pierce, Colorado with his wife Shana and their two boys. Their hobbies include camping, target shooting, bicycling, and trying to predict what the kids will get into next!

Eric Stromberg

Electrical Engineer/Instructor
Stromberg Engineering, Inc.
Los Alamos, NM
www.strombergengineering.com

Eric Stromberg worked as a journeyman electrician, before and during the time he attended college. When he graduated with a degree in Electrical Engineering in 1982, he took a job as an electronics technician. Eric became a licensed fire alarm installation superintendent and spent the next seven years installing and maintaining life safety systems in high-rise buildings.

In 1989, he went to work for Dow Chemical, where he designed power distribution systems for world-class industrial facilities. Eric began teaching *National Electrical Code* classes to engineers in 1997. He received his professional engineering license, for the State of Texas, in 2003 and, in 2005, started Stromberg Engineering.

In 2013, Eric retired from Dow Chemical and now lives in the mountains of northern New Mexico. Eric's oldest daughter, Ainsley, lives in Boston, Massachusetts with her husband Nathan. His son, Austin, is in the Air Force and is stationed at Minot, North Dakota. His youngest daughter, Brieanna, is a singer/songwriter who lives in Austin, Texas.

Notes

ARTICLE 90

INTRODUCTION TO THE *NATIONAL ELECTRICAL CODE*

Introduction to Article 90—Introduction to the *National Electrical Code*

Many *NEC* violations and misunderstandings wouldn't occur if people doing the work simply understood Article 90. For example, many people see *Code* requirements as performance standards. In fact, the *NEC* requirements are bare minimums for safety. This is exactly the stance electrical inspectors, insurance companies, and courts take when making a decision regarding electrical design or installation.

Article 90 opens by saying the *NEC* isn't intended as a design specification or instruction manual. The *National Electrical Code* has one purpose only, and that's the "practical safeguarding of persons and property from hazards arising from the use of electricity." The necessity of carefully studying the *NEC* rules can't be overemphasized, and the role of textbooks such as this one is to help in that undertaking. Understanding where to find the rules in the *Code* that apply to the installation is invaluable. Rules in several different articles often apply to even a simple installation.

Article 90 then describes the scope and arrangement of the *NEC*. The balance of this article provides the reader with information essential to understanding the *Code* rules.

Typically, electrical work requires you to understand the first four chapters of the *NEC* which apply generally, plus have a working knowledge of the Chapter 9 tables. That understanding begins with Article 90. Chapters 5, 6, and 7 make up a large portion of the *Code*, but they apply to special occupancies, special equipment, or other special conditions. They build on, modify, or amend the rules in the first four chapters. Chapter 8 contains the requirements for communications systems, such as telephone systems, antenna wiring, CATV, and network-powered broadband systems. Communications systems aren't subject to the general requirements of Chapters 1 through 4, or the special requirements of Chapters 5 through 7, unless there's a specific reference in Chapter 8 to a rule in Chapters 1 through 7.

90.1 Purpose of the *NEC*

(A) Practical Safeguarding. The purpose of the *NEC* is to ensure that electrical systems are installed in a manner that protects people and property by minimizing the risks associated with the use of electricity. It isn't a design specification standard or instruction manual for the untrained and unqualified. Figure 90–1

Author's Comment:

- The *Code* is intended to be used by those skilled and knowledgeable in electrical theory, electrical systems, construction, and the installation and operation of electrical equipment.

(B) Adequacy. The *Code* contains requirements considered necessary for a safe electrical installation. If an electrical system is installed in compliance with the *NEC*, it'll be essentially free from electrical hazards. The *Code* is a safety standard, not a design guide.

Figure 90–1

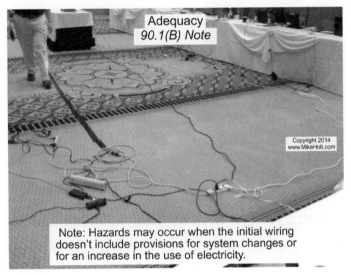

Figure 90–3

NEC requirements aren't intended to ensure the electrical installation will be efficient, convenient, adequate for good service, or suitable for future expansion. Specific items of concern, such as electrical energy management, maintenance, and power quality issues aren't within the scope of the *Code*. Figure 90–2

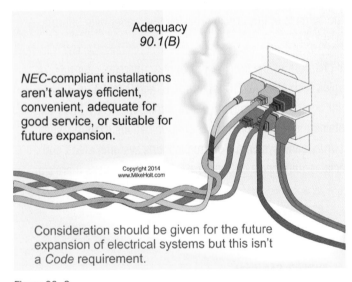

Figure 90–2

Note: Hazards in electrical systems often occur because circuits are overloaded or not properly installed in accordance with the *NEC*. These often occur if the initial wiring didn't provide reasonable provisions for system changes or for the increase in the use of electricity. Figure 90–3

Author's Comment:

■ See the definition of "Overload" in Article 100.

■ The *NEC* doesn't require electrical systems to be designed or installed to accommodate future loads. However, the electrical designer (typically an electrical engineer) is concerned with not only ensuring electrical safety (*Code* compliance), but also with ensuring the system meets the customers' needs, both of today and in the near future. To satisfy customers' needs, electrical systems are often designed and installed above the minimum requirements contained in the *NEC*. But just remember, if you're taking an exam, licensing exams are based on your understanding of the minimum *Code* requirements.

(C) Relation to International Standards. The requirements of the *NEC* address the fundamental safety principles contained in the International Electrotechnical Commission (IEC) standards, including protection against electric shock, adverse thermal effects, overcurrent, fault currents, and overvoltage. Figure 90–4

Author's Comment:

■ The *NEC* is used in Chile, Ecuador, Peru, and the Philippines. It's also the *Electrical Code* for Colombia, Costa Rica, Mexico, Panama, Puerto Rico, and Venezuela. Because of these adoptions, it's available in Spanish from the National Fire Protection Association, 617.770.3000, or www.NFPA.org.

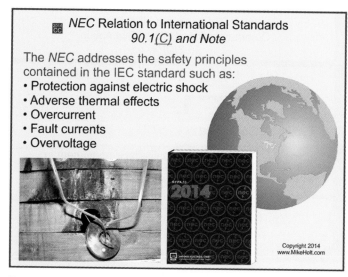

Figure 90–4

90.2 Scope of the *NEC*

(A) What Is Covered. The *NEC* contains requirements necessary for the proper installation of electrical conductors, equipment, cables, and raceways for power, signaling, fire alarm, optical cable, and communications systems for: Figure 90–5

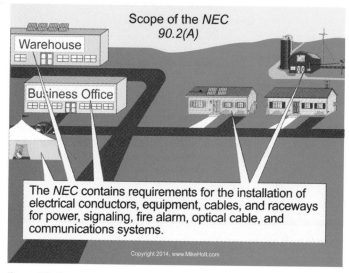

Figure 90–5

(1) Public and private premises, including buildings, mobile homes, recreational vehicles, and floating buildings. Figure 90–6

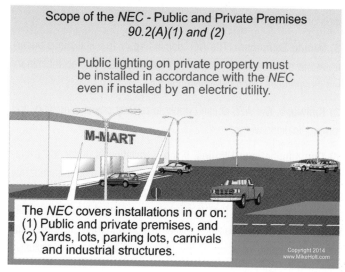

Figure 90–6

(2) Yards, lots, parking lots, carnivals, and industrial substations.

(3) Conductors and equipment connected to the utility supply.

(4) Installations used by an electric utility, such as office buildings, warehouses, garages, machine shops, recreational buildings, and other electric utility buildings that aren't an integral part of a utility's generating plant, substation, or control center. Figure 90–7

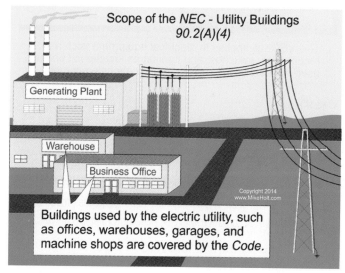

Figure 90–7

(B) What Isn't Covered. The *NEC* doesn't apply to:

(1) Transportation Vehicles. The *NEC* doesn't apply to installations in cars, trucks, boats, ships and watercraft, planes, electric trains, or underground mines.

(2) Mining Equipment. The *NEC* doesn't apply to installations underground in mines and self-propelled mobile surface mining machinery and its attendant electrical trailing cables.

(3) Railways. The *NEC* doesn't apply to railway power, signaling, and communications wiring.

(4) Communications Utilities. If the installation is under the exclusive control of the communications utility, the installation requirements of the *NEC* don't apply to the communications (telephone), Community Antenna Television (CATV), or network-powered broadband utility equipment located in building spaces used exclusively for these purposes, or located outdoors if the installation is under the exclusive control of the communications utility. Figure 90–8 and Figure 90–9

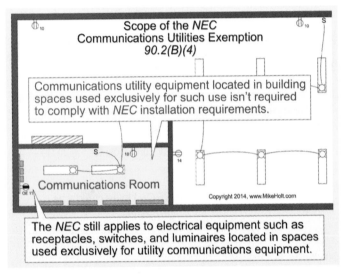

Figure 90–8

Author's Comment:

- Interior wiring for communications systems, not in building spaces used exclusively for these purposes, must be installed in accordance with the following Chapter 8 Articles:

  □ Telephone and Data, Article 800

  □ CATV, Article 820

  □ Network-Powered Broadband, Article 830

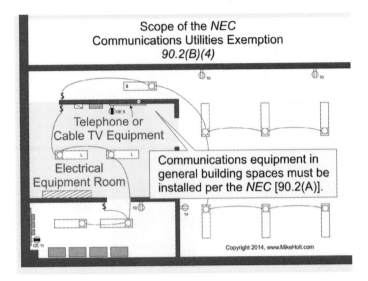

Figure 90–9

(5) Electric Utilities. The *NEC* doesn't apply to electrical installations under the exclusive control of an electric utility where such installations:

    a. Consist of utility installed service drops or service laterals under their exclusive control. Figure 90–10

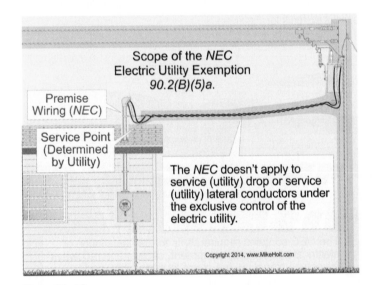

Figure 90–10

    b. Are on property owned or leased by the electric utility for the purpose of generation, transformation, transmission, distribution, or metering of electric energy. Figure 90–11

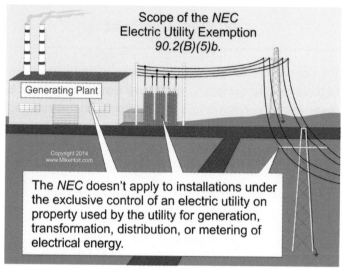

Figure 90–11

Author's Comment:

■ Luminaires located in legally established easements, or rights-of-way, such as at poles supporting transmission or distribution lines, are exempt from the *NEC*. However, if the electric utility provides site and public lighting on private property, then the installation must comply with the *Code* [90.2(A)(4)].

c. Are located on legally established easements, or rights-of-way. Figure 90–12

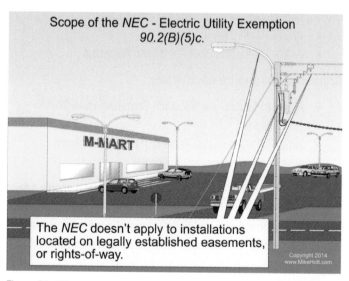

Figure 90–12

d. Are located by other written agreements either designated by or recognized by public service commissions, utility commissions, or other regulatory agencies having jurisdiction for such installations; limited to installations for the purpose of communications, metering, generation, control, transformation, transmission, or distribution of electric energy where legally established easements or rights-of-way can't be obtained. These installations are limited to federal lands, Native American reservations through the U.S. Department of the Interior Bureau of Indian Affairs, military bases, lands controlled by port authorities and state agencies and departments, and lands owned by railroads.

Note to 90.2(B)(4) and (5): Utilities include entities that install, operate, and maintain communications systems (telephone, CATV, Internet, satellite, or data services) or electric supply (generation, transmission, or distribution systems) and are designated or recognized by governmental law or regulation by public service/utility commissions. Utilities may be subject to compliance with codes and standards covering their regulated activities as adopted under governmental law or regulation.

90.3 *Code* Arrangement

The *Code* is divided into an introduction and nine chapters. Figure 90–13

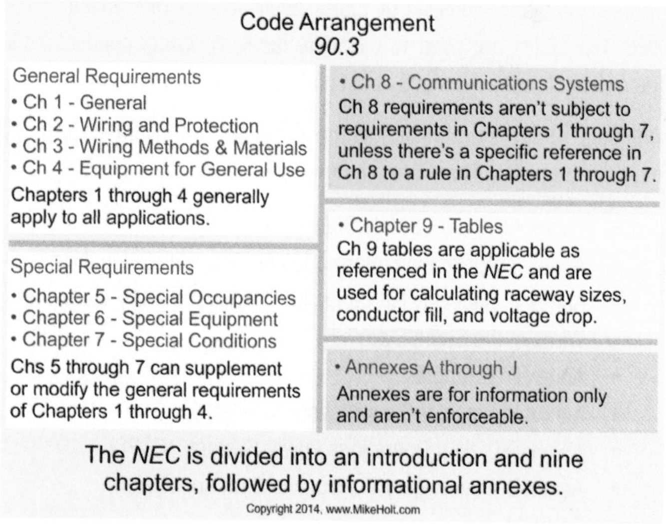

Code Arrangement
90.3

General Requirements
• Ch 1 - General
• Ch 2 - Wiring and Protection
• Ch 3 - Wiring Methods & Materials
• Ch 4 - Equipment for General Use
Chapters 1 through 4 generally apply to all applications.

Special Requirements
• Chapter 5 - Special Occupancies
• Chapter 6 - Special Equipment
• Chapter 7 - Special Conditions
Chs 5 through 7 can supplement or modify the general requirements of Chapters 1 through 4.

• Ch 8 - Communications Systems
Ch 8 requirements aren't subject to requirements in Chapters 1 through 7, unless there's a specific reference in Ch 8 to a rule in Chapters 1 through 7.

• Chapter 9 - Tables
Ch 9 tables are applicable as referenced in the *NEC* and are used for calculating raceway sizes, conductor fill, and voltage drop.

• Annexes A through J
Annexes are for information only and aren't enforceable.

The *NEC* is divided into an introduction and nine chapters, followed by informational annexes.
Copyright 2014, www.MikeHolt.com

Figure 90–13

General Requirements. The requirements contained in Chapters 1, 2, 3, and 4 apply to all installations.

Author's Comment:

■ These first four chapters may be thought of as the foundation for the rest of the *Code*, and are the main focus of this textbook.

Special Requirements. The requirements contained in Chapters 5, 6, and 7 apply to special occupancies, special equipment, or other special conditions. These chapters can supplement or modify the requirements in Chapters 1 through 4.

Communications Systems. Chapter 8 contains the requirements for communications systems, such as telephone systems, antenna wiring, CATV, and network-powered broadband systems. Communications systems aren't subject to the general requirements of Chapters 1 through 4, or the special requirements of Chapters 5 through 7, unless there's a specific reference in Chapter 8 to a rule in Chapters 1 through 7.

Author's Comment:

■ An example of how Chapter 8 works is in the rules for working space about equipment. The typical 3 ft working space isn't required in front of communications equipment, because Table 110.26(A)(1) isn't referenced in Chapter 8.

Tables. Chapter 9 consists of tables applicable as referenced in the *NEC*. The tables are used to calculate raceway sizing, conductor fill, the radius of raceway bends, and conductor voltage drop.

Annexes. Annexes aren't part of the *Code*, but are included for informational purposes. There are ten Annexes:

- Annex A. Product Safety Standards
- Annex B. Application Information for Ampacity Calculation
- Annex C. Raceway Fill Tables for Conductors and Fixture Wires of the Same Size
- Annex D. Examples
- Annex E. Types of Construction
- Annex F. Critical Operations Power Systems (COPS)
- Annex G. Supervisory Control and Data Acquisition (SCADA)
- Annex H. Administration and Enforcement
- Annex I. Recommended Tightening Torques
- Annex J. ADA Standards for Accessible Design

90.4 Enforcement

The *Code* is intended to be suitable for enforcement by governmental bodies that exercise legal jurisdiction over electrical installations for power, lighting, signaling circuits, and communications systems, such as: Figure 90–14

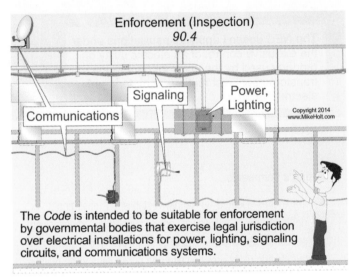

The *Code* is intended to be suitable for enforcement by governmental bodies that exercise legal jurisdiction over electrical installations for power, lighting, signaling circuits, and communications systems.

Figure 90–14

Signaling circuits which include:

- Article 725 Class 1, Class 2, and Class 3 Remote-Control, Signaling, and Power-Limited Circuits
- Article 760 Fire Alarm Systems
- Article 770 Optical Fiber Cables and Raceways

Communications systems which include:

- Article 810 Radio and Television Equipment (satellite dish and antenna)
- Article 820 Community Antenna Television and Radio Distribution Systems (coaxial cable)

The enforcement of the *NEC* is the responsibility of the authority having jurisdiction (AHJ), who is responsible for interpreting requirements, approving equipment and materials, waiving *Code* requirements, and ensuring equipment is installed in accordance with listing instructions.

Author's Comment:

■ See the definition of "Authority Having Jurisdiction" in Article 100.

Interpretation of the Requirements. The authority having jurisdiction is responsible for interpreting the *NEC*, but his or her decisions must be based on a specific *Code* requirement. If an installation is rejected, the authority having jurisdiction is legally responsible for informing the installer of the specific *NEC* rule that was violated. Figure 90–15

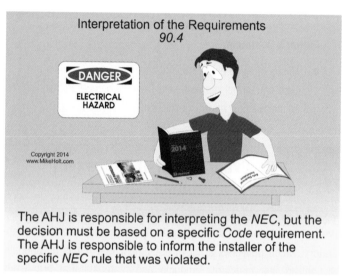

The AHJ is responsible for interpreting the *NEC*, but the decision must be based on a specific *Code* requirement. The AHJ is responsible to inform the installer of the specific *NEC* rule that was violated.

Figure 90–15

Author's Comment:

■ The art of getting along with the authority having jurisdiction consists of doing good work and knowing what the *Code* actually says (as opposed to what you only think it says). It's also useful to know how to choose your battles when the inevitable disagreement does occur.

Approval of Equipment and Materials. Only the authority having jurisdiction has authority to approve the installation of equipment and materials. Typically, the authority having jurisdiction will approve equipment listed by a product testing organization, such as Underwriters Laboratories, Inc. (UL). The *NEC* doesn't require all equipment to be listed, but many state and local AHJs do. See 90.7, 110.2, 110.3, and the definitions for "Approved," "Identified," "Labeled," and "Listed" in Article 100. Figure 90–16

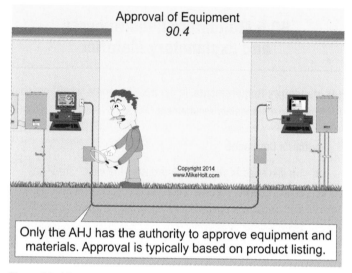

Only the AHJ has the authority to approve equipment and materials. Approval is typically based on product listing.

Figure 90–16

Author's Comment:

■ According to the *NEC*, the authority having jurisdiction determines the approval of equipment. This means he or she can reject an installation of listed equipment and can approve the use of unlisted equipment. Given our highly litigious society, approval of unlisted equipment is becoming increasingly difficult to obtain.

Approval of Alternate Means. By special permission, the authority having jurisdiction may approve alternate methods where it's assured equivalent safety can be achieved and maintained.

Author's Comment:

■ Special permission is defined in Article 100 as the written consent of the authority having jurisdiction.

Waiver of New Product Requirements. If the current *NEC* requires products that aren't yet available at the time the *Code* is adopted, the authority having jurisdiction can allow products that were acceptable in the previous *Code* to continue to be used.

Author's Comment:

■ Sometimes it takes years before testing laboratories establish product standards for new *NEC* requirements, and then it takes time before manufacturers can design, manufacture, and distribute those products to the marketplace.

90.5 Mandatory Requirements and Explanatory Material

(A) Mandatory Requirements. In the *NEC* the words "shall" or "shall not," indicate a mandatory requirement.

Author's Comment:

- For the ease of reading this textbook, the word "shall" has been replaced with the word "must," and the words "shall not" have been replaced with "must not." Remember that in many places, we'll paraphrase the *Code* instead of providing exact quotes, to make it easier to read and understand.

(B) Permissive Requirements. When the *Code* uses "shall be permitted" it means the identified actions are permitted but not required, and the authority having jurisdiction isn't permitted to restrict an installation from being completed in that manner. A permissive rule is often an exception to the general requirement.

Author's Comment:

- For ease of reading, the phrase "shall be permitted," as used in the *Code*, has been replaced in this textbook with the phrase "is permitted" or "are permitted."

(C) Explanatory Material. References to other standards or sections of the *NEC*, or information related to a *Code* rule, are included in the form of Informational Notes. Such notes are for information only and aren't enforceable as requirements of the *NEC*.

For example, Informational Note 4 in 210.19(A)(1) recommends that the voltage drop of a circuit not exceed 3 percent. This isn't a requirement; it's just a recommendation.

Author's Comment:

- For convenience and ease of reading in this textbook, Informational Notes will simply be identified as "Note."

- Informational Notes aren't enforceable, but Table Notes are. This textbook will call notes found in a table "Table Notes."

(D) Informative Annexes. Nonmandatory information annexes contained in the back of the *Code* book are for information only and aren't enforceable as requirements of the *NEC*.

90.6 Formal Interpretations

To promote uniformity of interpretation and application of the provisions of the *NEC*, formal interpretation procedures have been established and are found in the NFPA Regulations Governing Committee Projects.

Author's Comment:

- This is rarely done because it's a very time-consuming process, and formal interpretations from the NFPA aren't binding on the authority having jurisdiction.

90.7 Examination of Equipment for Product Safety

Product evaluation for safety is typically performed by a testing laboratory, which publishes a list of equipment that meets a nationally recognized test standard. Products and materials that are listed, labeled, or identified by a testing laboratory are generally approved by the authority having jurisdiction.

Author's Comment:

- See Article 100 for the definition of "Approved."

Except to detect alterations or damage, listed factory-installed internal wiring and construction of equipment needn't be inspected at the time of installation [300.1(B)]. Figure 90–17

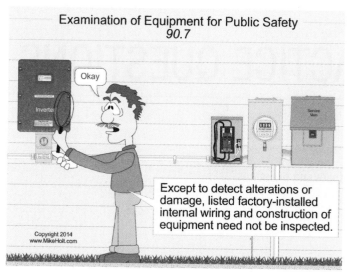

Examination of Equipment for Public Safety
90.7

Okay

Except to detect alterations or damage, listed factory-installed internal wiring and construction of equipment need not be inspected.

Figure 90–17

90.9 Units of Measurement

(B) Dual Systems of Units. Both the metric and inch-pound measurement systems are shown in the *NEC*, with the metric units appearing first and the inch-pound system immediately following in parentheses.

Author's Comment:

■ This is the standard practice in all NFPA standards, even though the U.S. construction industry uses inch-pound units of measurement. You'll need to be cautious when using the tables in the *Code* because the additional units can make the tables more complex and more difficult to read.

(D) Compliance. Installing electrical systems in accordance with the metric system or the inch-pound system is considered to comply with the *Code*.

ARTICLE 90 PRACTICE QUESTIONS

Please use the 2014 *Code* book to answer the following questions.

1. The *NEC* is _____.

   (a) intended to be a design manual
   (b) meant to be used as an instruction guide for untrained persons
   (c) for the practical safeguarding of persons and property
   (d) published by the Bureau of Standards

2. Compliance with the provisions of the *NEC* will result in _____.

   (a) good electrical service
   (b) an efficient electrical system
   (c) an electrical system essentially free from hazard
   (d) all of these

3. Hazards often occur because of _____.

   (a) overloading of wiring systems by methods or usage not in conformity with the *NEC*
   (b) initial wiring not providing for increases in the use of electricity
   (c) a and b
   (d) none of these

4. The *NEC* applies to the installation of _____.

   (a) electrical conductors and equipment within or on public and private buildings
   (b) outside conductors and equipment on the premises
   (c) optical fiber cables and raceways
   (d) all of these

5. The *NEC* does not cover electrical installations in ships, watercraft, railway rolling stock, aircraft, or automotive vehicles.

   (a) True
   (b) False

6. Installations of communications equipment that are under the exclusive control of communications utilities, and located outdoors or in building spaces used exclusively for such installations _____ covered by the *NEC*.

   (a) are
   (b) are sometimes
   (c) are not
   (d) may be

7. Utilities may be subject to compliance with codes and standards covering their regulated activities as adopted under governmental law or regulation.

   (a) True
   (b) False

8. Utilities may include entities that are designated or recognized by governmental law or regulation by public service/utility commissions.

   (a) True
   (b) False

9. Chapters 1 through 4 of the *NEC* apply _____.

    (a) generally to all electrical installations
    (b) only to special occupancies and conditions
    (c) only to special equipment and material
    (d) all of these

10. The authority having jurisdiction shall not be allowed to enforce any requirements of Chapter 7 (Special Conditions) or Chapter 8 (Communications Systems).

    (a) True
    (b) False

11. By special permission, the authority having jurisdiction may waive specific requirements in this *Code* where it is assured that equivalent objectives can be achieved by establishing and maintaining effective safety.

    (a) True
    (b) False

12. If the *NEC* requires new products that are not yet available at the time a new edition is adopted, the _____ may permit the use of the products that comply with the most recent previous edition of the *Code* adopted by that jurisdiction.

    (a) electrical engineer
    (b) master electrician
    (c) authority having jurisdiction
    (d) permit holder

13. When the *Code* uses "_____," it means the identified actions are allowed but not required, and they may be options or alternative methods.

    (a) shall
    (b) shall not
    (c) shall be permitted
    (d) a or b

14. Nonmandatory Informative Annexes contained in the back of the *Code* book _____.

    (a) are for information only
    (b) aren't enforceable as a requirement of the *Code*
    (c) are enforceable as a requirement of the *Code*
    (d) a and b

Notes

GENERAL REQUIREMENTS FOR WIRING METHODS AND MATERIALS

Introduction to Article 300—General Requirements for Wiring Methods and Materials

Article 300 contains the general requirements for all wiring methods included in the *NEC*. However, the article doesn't apply to communications systems, which are covered in Chapter 8, except when Article 300 is specifically referenced in Chapter 8.

This article is primarily concerned with how to install, route, splice, protect, and secure conductors and raceways. How well you conform to the requirements of Article 300 will generally be evident in the finished work, because many of the requirements tend to determine the appearance of the installation.

Because of this, it's often easy to spot Article 300 problems if you're looking for *Code* violations. For example, you can easily see when someone runs an equipment grounding conductor outside a raceway instead of grouping all conductors of a circuit together, as required by 300.3(B).

A good understanding of Article 300 will start you on the path to correctly installing the wiring methods included in Chapter 3. Be sure to carefully consider the accompanying illustrations, and refer to the definitions in Article 100 as needed.

Part I. General

300.4 Protection Against Physical Damage

Conductors, raceways, and cables must be protected against physical damage [110.27(B)].

(D) Cables and Raceways Parallel to Framing Members and Furring Strips. Cables or raceways run parallel to framing members or furring strips must be protected if they're likely to be penetrated by nails or screws, by installing the wiring method so it isn't less than 1¼ in. from the nearest edge of the framing member or furring strip. If the edge of the framing member or furring strip is less than 1¼ in. away, a ¹⁄₁₆ in. thick steel plate of sufficient length and width must be installed to protect the wiring method from screws and nails. Figure 300–1

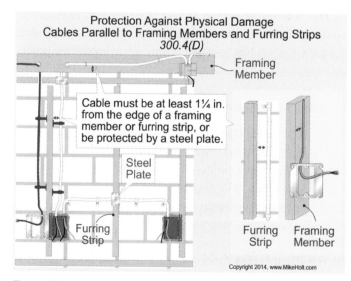

Figure 300–1

Author's Comment:

■ This rule doesn't apply to control, signaling, and communications cables, but similar requirements are contained in Chapters 6, 7, and 8 as follows:

☐ CATV Coaxial Cable, 820.24

☐ Communications Cable, 800.24

☐ Control and Signaling Cable, 725.24

☐ Optical Fiber Cable, 770.24

☐ Fire Alarm Cable, 760.8

☐ Audio Cable, 640.6(B)

Ex 1: Protection isn't required for rigid metal conduit, intermediate metal conduit, PVC conduit, or electrical metallic tubing.

Ex 2: For concealed work in finished buildings, or finished panels for prefabricated buildings if such supporting is impracticable, the cables can be fished between access points.

Ex 3: A listed and marked steel plate less than ¹⁄₁₆ in. thick that provides equal or better protection against nail or screw penetration is permitted.

300.11 Securing and Supporting

(A) Secured in Place. Raceways, cable assemblies, and enclosures must be securely fastened in place. The ceiling-support wires or ceiling grid must not be used to support raceways and cables (power, signaling, or communications). However, independent support wires that are secured at both ends and provide secure support are permitted. Figure 300–2

Author's Comment:

■ Outlet boxes [314.23(D)] and luminaires can be secured to the suspended-ceiling grid if securely fastened to the ceiling-framing members by mechanical means such as bolts, screws, or rivets, or by the use of clips or other securing means identified for use with the type of ceiling-framing member(s) used [410.36(B)].

(1) Fire-Rated Ceiling Assembly. Electrical wiring within the cavity of a fire-rated floor-ceiling or roof-ceiling assembly can be supported by independent support wires attached to the ceiling assembly. The independent support wires must be distinguishable from the suspended-ceiling support wires by color, tagging, or other effective means.

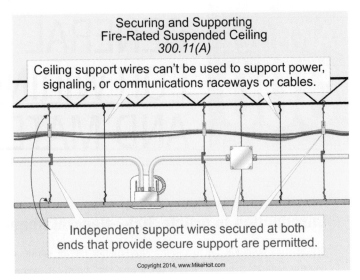

Figure 300–2

(2) Nonfire-Rated Ceiling Assembly. Wiring in a nonfire-rated floor-ceiling or roof-ceiling assembly can be supported by independent support wires attached to the ceiling assembly. The independent support wires must be distinguishable from the suspended-ceiling support wires by color, tagging, or other effective means. Figure 300–3

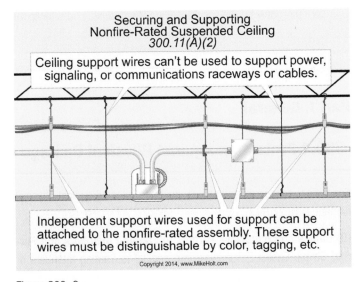

Figure 300–3

(B) Raceways Used for Support. Raceways must not be used as a means of support for other raceways, cables, or nonelectrical equipment, except as permitted in (1) through (3). Figure 300–4

(1) Identified. If the raceway or means of support is identified as a means of support.

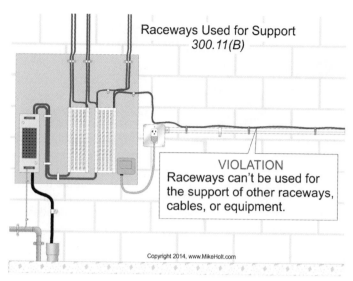

Figure 300–4

(2) Class 2 and 3 Circuits. Class 2 and 3 cable can be supported by the raceway that supplies power to the equipment controlled by the Class 2 or 3 circuit. Figure 300–5

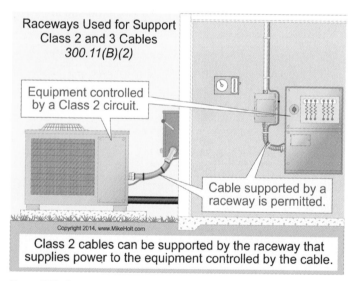

Figure 300–5

(3) Boxes Supported by Raceways. Raceways are permitted as a means of support for threaded boxes and conduit bodies in accordance with 314.23(E) and (F), or to support luminaires in accordance with 410.36(E).

300.17 Raceway Sizing

Raceways must be large enough to permit the installation and removal of conductors without damaging the conductor's insulation.

Author's Comment:

■ When all conductors in a raceway are the same size and of the same insulation type, the number of conductors permitted can be determined by Annex C.

> **Question:** How many 12 THHN conductors can be installed in trade size ¾ electrical metallic tubing? Figure 300–6
>
> (a) 12   (b) 13   c) 14   (d) 16
>
> **Answer:** (d) 16 conductors [Annex C, Table C1]

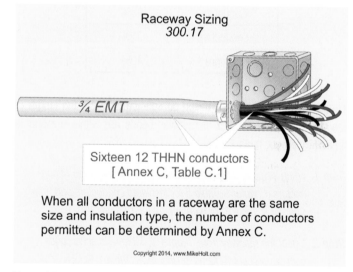

Figure 300–6

Author's Comment:

■ When different size conductors are installed in a raceway, conductor fill is limited to the percentages in Table 1 of Chapter 9. Figure 300–7

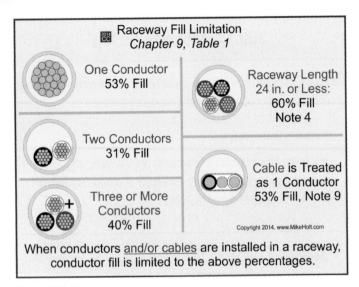

Figure 300–7

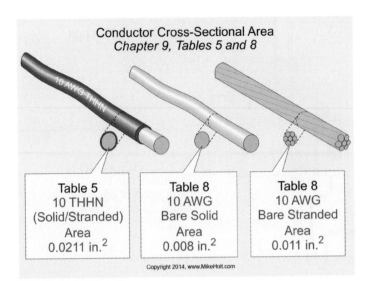

Figure 300–8

Table 1, Chapter 9	
Number	**Percent Fill**
1 Conductor	53%
2 Conductors	31%
3 or more	40%

The above percentages are based on conditions where the length of the conductor and number of raceway bends are within reasonable limits [Chapter 9, Table 1, Note 1].

Step 1: *When sizing a raceway, first determine the total area of conductors (Chapter 9, Table 5 for insulated conductors and Chapter 9, Table 8 for bare conductors).* Figure 300–8

Step 2: *Select the raceway from Chapter 9, Table 4, in accordance with the percent fill listed in Chapter 9, Table 1.* Figure 300–9

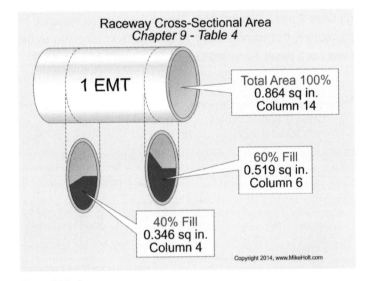

Figure 300–9

Question: *What trade size Schedule 40 PVC conduit is required for the following conductors?* Figure 300–10

3—500 THHN

1—250 THHN

1—3 THHN

(a) 2   *(b) 3*   *(c) 4*   *(d) 6*

Answer: *(b) 3*

Step 1: *Determine the total area of conductors [Chapter 9, Table 5]:*

500 THHN	*0.7073 x 3 =*	*2.1219 in.²*
250 THHN	*0.3970 x 1 =*	*0.3970 in.²*
3 THHN	*0.0973 x 1 =*	*+ 0.0973 in.²*
Total Area =		*2.6162 in.²*

Step 2: *Select the raceway at 40 percent fill [Chapter 9, Table 4]:*

Trade size 3 Schedule 40 PVC = 2.907 sq in. of conductor fill at 40%.

Raceway Sizing
300.17

Schedule 40 PVC

Step 1. Determine the conductor area, Chapter 9, Table 5.

500 kcmil = 0.7073 in.² x 3 conductors = 2.1219 in.²
250 kcmil = 0.3970 in.² x 1 conductor   = 0.3970 in.²
3 AWG = 0.0973 in.² x 1 conductor   = 0.0973 in.²
Total area of the conductors = 2.6162 in.²

Step 2. Size the raceway at 40% fill, Chapter 9, Table 4.

Trade Size 3 PVC at 40 percent fill = 2.907 in.²   Copyright 2014
www.MikeHolt.com

Figure 300–10

300.21 Spread of Fire or Products of Combustion

Electrical circuits and equipment must be installed in such a way that the spread of fire or products of combustion won't be substantially increased. Openings into or through fire-rated walls, floors, and ceilings for electrical equipment must be fire-stopped using methods approved by the authority having jurisdiction to maintain the fire-resistance rating of the fire-rated assembly. Figure 300–11

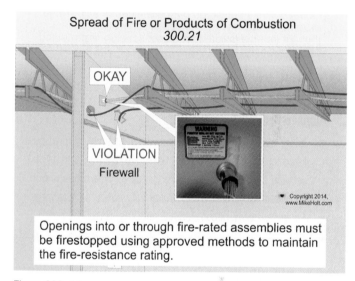

Spread of Fire or Products of Combustion
300.21

OKAY

VIOLATION

Firewall

Copyright 2014,
www.MikeHolt.com

Openings into or through fire-rated assemblies must be firestopped using approved methods to maintain the fire-resistance rating.

Figure 300–11

Author's Comment:

■ Fire-stopping materials are listed for the specific types of wiring methods and the construction of the assembly that they penetrate.

Note: Directories of electrical construction materials published by qualified testing laboratories contain listing and installation restrictions necessary to maintain the fire-resistive rating of assemblies. Outlet boxes must have a horizontal separation not less than 24 in. when installed in a fire-rated assembly, unless an outlet box is listed for closer spacing or protected by fire-resistant "putty pads" in accordance with manufacturer's instructions. Figure 300–12

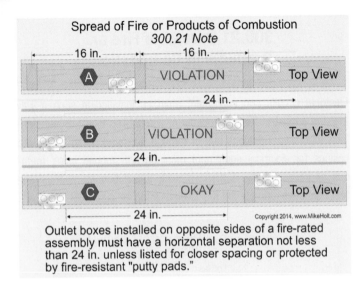

Spread of Fire or Products of Combustion
300.21 Note

Outlet boxes installed on opposite sides of a fire-rated assembly must have a horizontal separation not less than 24 in. unless listed for closer spacing or protected by fire-resistant "putty pads."

Figure 300–12

Author's Comment:

■ Boxes installed in fire-resistance-rated assemblies must be listed for the purpose. If steel boxes are used, they must be secured to the framing member, so cut-in type boxes aren't permitted (UL White Book, *Guide Information for Electrical Equipment,* www.ul.com/regulators/2008_WhiteBook.pdf).

■ This rule also applies to control, signaling, and communications cables or raceways.

  □ CATV, 820.26

  □ Communications, 800.26

  □ Control and Signaling, 725.25

  □ Fire Alarm, 760.3(A)

  □ Optical Fiber, 770.26

  □ Sound Systems, 640.3(A)

300.22 Wiring in Ducts and Plenums Spaces

 Scan the QR code for a video clip of Mike explaining this topic; this is a sample from the DVDs that accompany this textbook.

The provisions of this section apply to the installation and uses of electrical wiring and equipment in ducts used for dust, loose stock, or vapor removal; ducts specifically fabricated for environmental air, and spaces used for environmental air (plenums).

(A) Ducts Used for Dust, Loose Stock, or Vapor. Ducts that transport dust, loose stock, or vapors must not have any wiring method installed within them. Figure 300–13

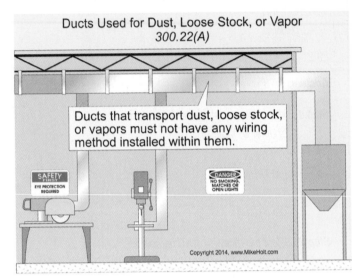

Ducts Used for Dust, Loose Stock, or Vapor
300.22(A)

Ducts that transport dust, loose stock, or vapors must not have any wiring method installed within them.

Figure 300–13

(B) Ducts Specifically Fabricated for Environmental Air. If necessary for direct action upon, or sensing of, the contained air, Type MC cable that has a smooth or corrugated impervious metal sheath without an overall nonmetallic covering, electrical metallic tubing, flexible metallic tubing, intermediate metal conduit, or rigid metal conduit without an overall nonmetallic covering can be installed in ducts specifically fabricated to transport environmental air. Flexible metal conduit in lengths not exceeding 4 ft can be used to connect physically adjustable equipment and devices within the fabricated duct.

Equipment is only permitted within the duct specifically fabricated to transport environmental air if necessary for the direct action upon, or sensing of, the contained air. Equipment, devices, and/or illumination are only permitted to be installed in the duct if necessary to facilitate maintenance and repair. Figure 300–14

(C) Other Spaces Used for Environmental Air (Plenums). This section applies to spaces used for air-handling purposes, but not fabricated for environmental air-handling purposes. This requirement doesn't apply to habitable rooms or areas of buildings, the prime purpose of which isn't air handling. Figure 300–15

Wiring in Ducts Specifically Fabricated for Environmental Air
300.22(B)

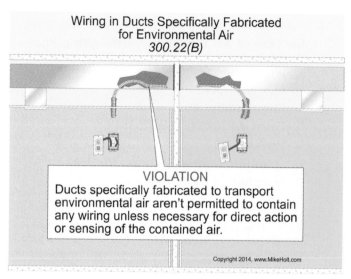

VIOLATION
Ducts specifically fabricated to transport environmental air aren't permitted to contain any wiring unless necessary for direct action or sensing of the contained air.

Copyright 2014, www.MikeHolt.com

Figure 300–14

Other Spaces Used as a Plenum Space
300.22(C) Note 1

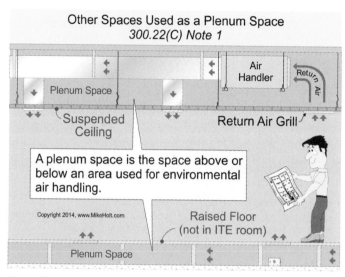

A plenum space is the space above or below an area used for environmental air handling.

Copyright 2014, www.MikeHolt.com

Figure 300–16

Other Spaces Used as a Plenum Space
300.22(C)

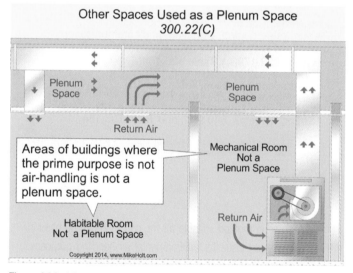

Areas of buildings where the prime purpose is not air-handling is not a plenum space.

Mechanical Room Not a Plenum Space

Habitable Room Not a Plenum Space

Copyright 2014, www.MikeHolt.com

Figure 300–15

Note 1: The spaces above a suspended ceiling or below a raised floor used for environmental air are examples of the type of space to which this section applies. Figure 300–16

Note 2: The phrase "other space used for environmental air (plenums)" correlates with the term "plenum" in NFPA 90A, *Standard for the Installation of Air-Conditioning and Ventilating Systems*, and other mechanical codes where the ceiling is used for return air purposes, as well as some other air-handling spaces.

Ex: In a dwelling unit, this section doesn't apply to the space between joists or studs where the wiring passes through that space perpendicular to the long dimension of that space. Figure 300–17

Other Spaces Used as a Plenum Space - Dwelling
300.22(C) Ex

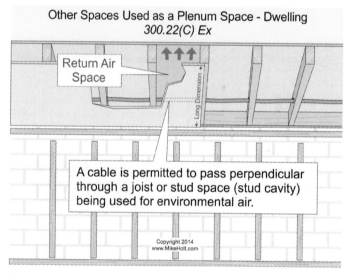

A cable is permitted to pass perpendicular through a joist or stud space (stud cavity) being used for environmental air.

Copyright 2014 www.MikeHolt.com

Figure 300–17

(1) Wiring Methods. Electrical metallic tubing, rigid metal conduit, intermediate metal conduit, armored cable, metal-clad cable without a nonmetallic cover, and flexible metal conduit can be installed in plenum spaces. If accessible, surface metal raceways or metal wireways with metal covers can be installed in a plenum space. Figure 300–18

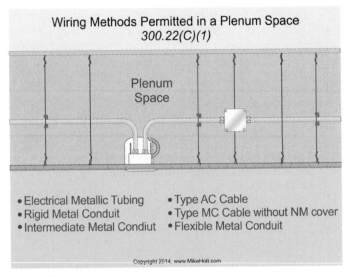

Figure 300–18

Cable ties for securing and supporting must be listed as having adequate fire resistant and low smoke producing characteristics. Figure 300–19

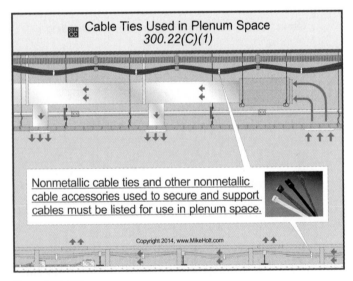

Figure 300–19

Author's Comment:

■ PVC conduit [Article 352], electrical nonmetallic tubing [Article 362], liquidtight flexible conduit, and nonmetallic cables aren't permitted to be installed in plenum spaces because they give off deadly toxic fumes when burned or superheated.

■ Plenum-rated control, signaling, and communications cables and raceways are permitted in plenum spaces: Figure 300–20

  □ CATV, 820.179(A)
  □ Communications, 800.21
  □ Control and Signaling, Table 725.154
  □ Fire Alarm, 760.7
  □ Optical Fiber Cables and Raceways, 770.113(C)
  □ Sound Systems, 640.9(C) and Table 725.154

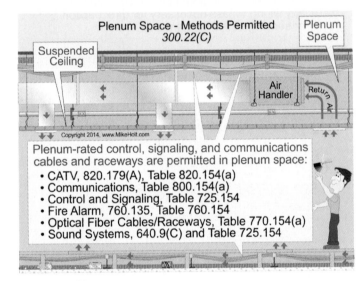

Figure 300–20

■ Any wiring method suitable for the condition can be used in a space not used for environmental air-handling purposes. Figure 300–21

(2) Cable Tray Systems.

(a) Metal Cable Tray Systems. Metal cable tray systems can be installed to support the wiring methods and equipment permitted by this section. Figure 300–22

(3) Equipment. Electrical equipment with metal enclosures is permitted to be installed in plenum spaces. Figure 300–23

Figure 300–21

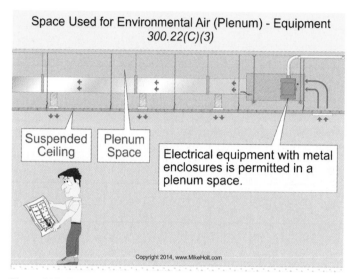

Figure 300–23

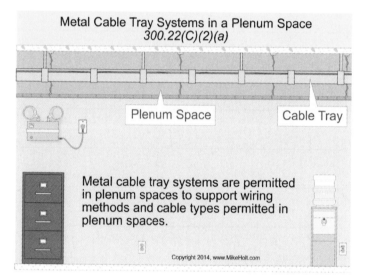

Figure 300–22

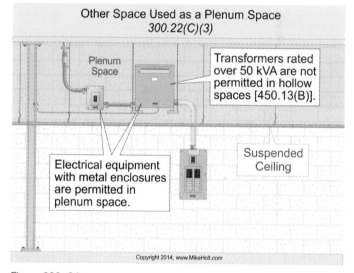

Figure 300–24

Author's Comment:

■ Examples of electrical equipment permitted in plenum spaces are air-handlers, junction boxes, and dry-type transformers; however, transformers must not be rated over 50 kVA when located in hollow spaces [450.13(B)]. Figure 300–24

Mike Holt's Understanding 2014 NEC Requirements for Limited Energy & Communications Systems

ARTICLE 300 PRACTICE QUESTIONS

Please use the 2014 *Code* book to answer the following questions.

1. Where cables or nonmetallic raceways are installed through bored holes in joists, rafters, or wood members, holes shall be bored so that the edge of the hole is _____ the nearest edge of the wood member.

   (a) not less than 1¼ in. from
   (b) immediately adjacent to
   (c) not less than ¹⁄₁₆ in. from
   (d) 90° away from

2. Cables laid in wood notches require protection against nails or screws by using a steel plate at least _____ thick, installed before the building finish is applied.

   (a) ¹⁄₁₆ in.
   (b) ⅛ in.
   (c) ¼ in.
   (d) ½ in.

3. Where Type NM cable passes through factory or field openings in metal members, it shall be protected by _____ bushings or _____ grommets that cover metal edges.

   (a) approved
   (b) identified
   (c) listed
   (d) none of these

4. Where Type NM cables pass through cut or drilled slots or holes in metal members, the cable shall be protected by _____ which are installed in the opening prior to the installation of the cable and which securely cover all metal edges.

   (a) listed bushings
   (b) listed grommets
   (c) plates
   (d) a or b

5. Where nails or screws are likely to penetrate nonmetallic-sheathed cable or ENT installed through metal framing members, a steel sleeve, steel plate, or steel clip not less than _____ in thickness shall be used to protect the cable or tubing.

   (a) ¹⁄₁₆ in.
   (b) ⅛ in.
   (c) ½ in.
   (d) ¾ in.

6. Wiring methods installed behind panels that allow access shall be _____ according to their applicable articles.

   (a) supported
   (b) painted
   (c) in a metal raceway
   (d) all of these

7. Where cables and nonmetallic raceways are installed parallel to framing members, the nearest outside surface of the cable or raceway shall be _____ the nearest edge of the framing member where nails or screws are likely to penetrate.

   (a) not less than 1¼ in. from
   (b) immediately adjacent to
   (c) not less than ¹⁄₁₆ in. from
   (d) 90°away from

8. A cable, raceway, or box installed under metal-corrugated sheet roof decking shall be supported so the top of the cable, raceway, or box is not less than _____ from the lowest surface of the roof decking to the top of the cable, raceway, or box.

   (a) ½ in.
   (b) 1 in.
   (c) 1½ in.
   (d) 2 in.

9. When installed under metal-corrugated sheet roof decking, cables, raceways, and enclosures are permitted in concealed locations of metal-corrugated sheet decking type roofing if they are at least 2 in. away from a structural support member.

   (a) True
   (b) False

10. When installed under metal-corrugated sheet roof decking, the rules for spacing from roof decking apply equally to rigid metal conduit and intermediate metal conduit.

    (a) True
    (b) False

11. Where raceways contain insulated circuit conductors _____ AWG and larger, the conductors shall be protected from abrasion during and after installation by a fitting that provides a smooth, rounded insulating surface.

    (a) 8
    (b) 6
    (c) 4
    (d) 2

12. A listed expansion/deflection fitting or other approved means must be used where a raceway crosses a _____ intended for expansion, contraction or deflection used in buildings, bridges, parking garages, or other structures.

    (a) junction box
    (b) structural joint
    (c) cable tray
    (d) unistrut hanger

13. Raceways, cable assemblies, boxes, cabinets, and fittings shall be securely fastened in place.

    (a) True
    (b) False

14. Where independent support wires of a ceiling assembly are used to support raceways, cable assemblies, or boxes above a ceiling, they shall be secured at _____ ends.

    (a) one
    (b) both
    (c) a or b
    (d) none of these

15. Electrical wiring within the cavity of a fire-rated floor-ceiling or roof-ceiling assembly shall not be supported by the ceiling assembly or ceiling support wires.

    (a) True
    (b) False

16. The independent support wires for supporting electrical wiring methods in a fire-rated ceiling assembly shall be distinguishable from fire-rated suspended-ceiling framing support wires by _____.

    (a) color
    (b) tagging
    (c) other effective means
    (d) any of these

17. Independent support wires used for the support of electrical raceways and cables within nonfire-rated assemblies shall be distinguishable from the suspended-ceiling framing support wires.

    (a) True
    (b) False

18. Raceways can be used as a means of support of Class 2 circuit conductors or cables that connect to the same equipment.

    (a) True
    (b) False

19. The number and size of conductors permitted in a raceway is limited to _____.

    (a) permit heat to dissipate
    (b) prevent damage to insulation during installation
    (c) prevent damage to insulation during removal of conductors
    (d) all of these

20. Electrical installations in hollow spaces, vertical shafts, and ventilation or air-handling ducts shall be made so that the possible spread of fire or products of combustion is not _____.

    (a) substantially increased
    (b) allowed
    (c) inherent
    (d) possible

21. Openings around electrical penetrations into or through fire-resistant-rated walls, partitions, floors, or ceilings shall _____ to maintain the fire-resistance rating.

    (a) be documented
    (b) not be permitted
    (c) be firestopped using approved methods
    (d) be enlarged

22. No wiring of any type shall be installed in ducts used to transport _____.

    (a) dust
    (b) flammable vapors
    (c) loose stock
    (d) all of these

23. Equipment and devices shall only be permitted within ducts or plenum chambers specifically fabricated to transport environmental air if necessary for their direct action upon, or sensing of, the _____.

    (a) contained air
    (b) air quality
    (c) air temperature
    (d) none of these

24. The space above a hung ceiling used for environmental air-handling purposes is an example of _____, and the wiring limitations of _____ apply.

    (a) a specifically fabricated duct used for environmental air, 300.22(B)
    (b) other space used for environmental air (plenum), 300.22(C)
    (c) a supply duct used for environmental air, 300.22(B)
    (d) none of these

25. Wiring methods permitted in the ceiling areas used for environmental air include _____.

    (a) electrical metallic tubing
    (b) FMC of any length
    (c) RMC without an overall nonmetallic covering
    (d) all of these

26. _____ shall be permitted to support the wiring methods and equipment permitted to be used in other spaces used for environmental air (plenum).

    (a) Metal cable tray systems
    (b) Nonmetallic wireways
    (c) PVC conduit
    (d) Surface nonmetallic raceways

27. Electrical equipment with _____ and having adequate fire-resistant and low-smoke-producing characteristics can be installed within an air-handling space (plenum).

    (a) a metal enclosure
    (b) a nonmetallic enclosure listed for use within an air-handling (plenum) space
    (c) any type of enclosure
    (d) a or b

ARTICLE 725

REMOTE-CONTROL, SIGNALING, AND POWER-LIMITED CIRCUITS

Introduction to Article 725—Remote-Control, Signaling, and Power-Limited Circuits

Circuits that fall under Article 725 are remote-control, signaling, and power-limited circuits that aren't an integral part of a device or appliance. This article includes circuits for burglar alarms, access control, sound, nurse call, intercoms, some computer networks, some lighting dimmer controls, and some low-voltage industrial controls.

Let's take a quick look at the types of circuits:

- A remote-control circuit controls other circuits through a relay or solid-state device, such as a motion-activated security lighting circuit.
- A signaling circuit provides output that's a signal or indicator, such as a buzzer, flashing light, or annunciator.
- A power-limited circuit is a circuit supplied by a transformer or other power source that limits the amount of power to provide safety from electrical shock and/or fire ignition.

The purpose of Article 725 is to allow for the fact that these circuits "are characterized by usage and power limitations that differentiate them from electrical power circuits" [725.1 Note]. This article provides alternative requirements for minimum conductor sizes, overcurrent protection, insulation requirements, wiring methods, and materials.

Article 725 consists of four parts. Part I provides general information, Part II pertains to Class 1 circuits, Part III addresses Class 2 and Class 3 circuits, while Part IV focuses on listing requirements. The key to understanding and applying each of these parts is in knowing the voltage and energy levels of the circuits, the wiring method involved, and the purpose(s) of the circuit.

Part I. General

725.1 Scope

Article 725 contains the requirements for remote-control, signaling, and power-limited circuits that aren't an integral part of a device or appliance.

Note: These circuits have electrical power and voltage limitations that differentiate them from electrical power circuits. Alternative requirements are given with regard to minimum conductor sizes, overcurrent protection, insulation requirements, wiring methods, and materials.

Author's Comment:

- To understand when to apply the requirements of Article 725 for control, signaling, and power-limited circuits, you must understand the following Article 100 Definitions:

    □ **Remote-Control Circuit.** Any electrical circuit that controls another circuit through a relay or equivalent device is a remote-control circuit. An example is the 120V circuit that operates the coil of a motor starter or lighting contactor, or the 24V circuit for a garage door opener.

☐ **Signaling Circuit.** Any electrical circuit that energizes signaling equipment is a signaling circuit. Examples include doorbells, buzzers, signal lights, annunciators, burglar alarms, and other detection indication or alarm devices.

725.2 Definitions

 Scan the QR code for a video clip of Mike explaining this topic; this is a sample from the DVDs that accompany this textbook.

Abandoned Cable. A cable that isn't terminated to equipment and not identified for future use with a tag.

Author's Comment:

- Section 725.25 requires the accessible portion of abandoned cables to be removed.

Class 1 Circuit. That wiring system between the load side of the Class 1 circuit overcurrent device and the connected equipment such as relays, controllers, lights, audible devices, and so forth. Figure 725–1

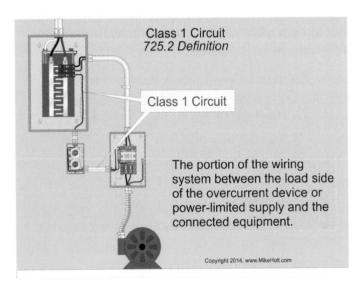

Figure 725–1

Author's Comment:

- Class 1 nonpower-limited circuits can operate at up to 600V and the power output isn't limited [725.41(B)].

Class 2 Circuit. The portion of the wiring system between the load side of a Class 2 power supply and the connected Class 2 equipment. Class 2 circuits are rendered safe by limiting the power supply to 100 VA for circuits that operate at 30V or less, and the current to 5 mA for circuits over 30V [Chapter 9, Table 11(A)]. Figure 725–2

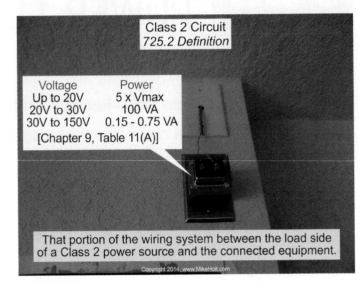

Figure 725–2

Author's Comment:

- Class 2 circuits typically include wiring for low-energy, low-voltage loads such as thermostats, programmable controllers, burglar alarms, and security systems. This type of circuit also includes twisted-pair or coaxial cable that interconnects computers for Local Area Networks (LANs) and programmable controller I/O circuits [725.121(A)(3) and 725.121(A)(4)].

Class 3 Circuit. The portion of the wiring system between the load side of a Class 3 power supply and the connected Class 3 equipment. Figure 725–3

Author's Comment:

- Class 3 circuits are used when the power demand exceeds 0.50 VA, but not more than 100 VA, for circuits over 30V [Chapter 9, Table 11(A)].

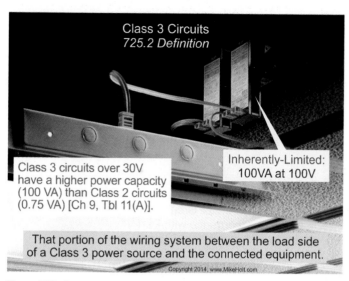

Class 3 Circuits
725.2 Definition

Class 3 circuits over 30V have a higher power capacity (100 VA) than Class 2 circuits (0.75 VA) [Ch 9, Tbl 11(A)].

Inherently-Limited: 100VA at 100V

That portion of the wiring system between the load side of a Class 3 power source and the connected equipment.

Copyright 2014, www.MikeHolt.com

Figure 725–3

725.3 Other Articles

Only those sections contained in Article 300 specifically referenced in this article apply to Class 1, 2, and 3 circuits.

Author's Comment:

■ Boxes or other enclosures aren't required for Class 2 or Class 3 splices or terminations because Article 725 doesn't reference 300.15, which contains those requirements. Figure 725–4

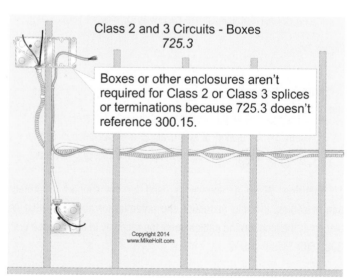

Class 2 and 3 Circuits - Boxes
725.3

Boxes or other enclosures aren't required for Class 2 or Class 3 splices or terminations because 725.3 doesn't reference 300.15.

Copyright 2014
www.MikeHolt.com

Figure 725–4

(A) Number and Size of Conductors in a Raceway. The number and size of conductors or cables in a raceway are limited in accordance with 300.17.

Author's Comment:

■ Raceways must be large enough to permit the installation and removal of conductors without damaging conductor insulation.

■ When all conductors in a raceway are the same size and insulation, the number of conductors permitted can be found in Annex C for the raceway type.

Question: *How many 18 TFFN fixture wires can be installed in trade size ½ electrical metallic tubing?* Figure 725–5

(a) 22   *(b) 26*   *(c) 30*   *(d) 40*

Answer: *(a) 22 conductors [Annex C, Table C.1]*

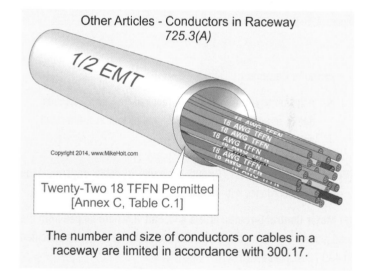

Other Articles - Conductors in Raceway
725.3(A)

1/2 EMT

18 AWG TFFN
18 AWG TFFN
18 AWG TFFN
18 AWG TFFN

Copyright 2014, www.MikeHolt.com

Twenty-Two 18 TFFN Permitted
[Annex C, Table C.1]

The number and size of conductors or cables in a raceway are limited in accordance with 300.17.

Figure 725–5

(B) Spread of Fire or Products of Combustion. Class 1, 2, and 3 circuits installed through fire-resistant-rated walls, partitions, floors, or ceilings must be firestopped to limit the possible spread of fire or products of combustion in accordance with the specific instructions supplied by the manufacturer for the specific type of cable and construction material (drywall, brick, and so on) [300.21]. Figure 725–6

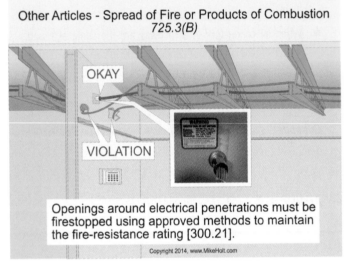

Figure 725–6

Author's Comment:

- Although boxes aren't typically required for Class 2 circuits, one is required for a Class 2 device located in a fire-rated assembly.

(E) Cable Trays. Class 1, 2, and 3 circuits in cable trays must be installed in accordance with Article 392.

(F) Motor Control Circuits. Article 430, Part VI, where tapped from the load side of the motor branch-circuit protective device(s) as specified in 430.72(A). Figure 725–7

(H) Raceways Exposed to Different Temperatures. If a raceway is subjected to different temperatures, and where condensation is known to be a problem, the raceway must be filled with a material approved by the authority having jurisdiction that will prevent the circulation of warm air to a colder section of the raceway. An explosionproof seal isn't required for this purpose [300.7(A)]. Figure 725–8

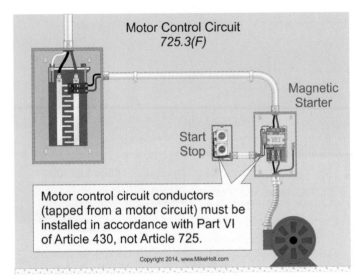

Figure 725–7

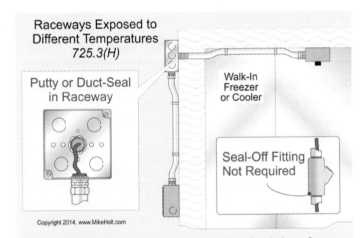

Raceways must be sealed to prevent the circulation of warm air to a colder section of the raceway or sleeve [300.7(A)].

Figure 725–8

Author's Comment:

- This raceway seal is one that's approved by the AHJ to prevent the circulation of warm air to a cooler section of the raceway, and isn't the same thing as an explosionproof seal.

(J) Bushing. When a raceway is used for the support or protection of cables, a fitting to reduce the potential for abrasion must be placed at the location the cables enter the raceway in accordance with 300.15(C). Figure 725–9

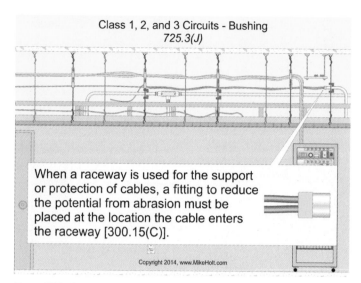

Figure 725–9

(L) Corrosive, Damp, or Wet Locations. Where installed in corrosive, damp, or wet locations, Class 2 and Class 3 cables must be identified for the location, in accordance with 110.11 and 310.10(G). Conductors and cables installed in underground raceways, or in raceways aboveground in wet locations, must also be identified for wet locations, in accordance with 300.5(B). Where corrosion may occur, the requirements of 300.6 must be used.

725.21 Electrical Equipment Behind Access Panels

Access to equipment must not be prohibited by an accumulation of cables that prevent the removal of suspended-ceiling panels.

Author's Comment:

■ Cables must be located so that the suspended-ceiling panels can be moved to provide access to electrical equipment.

725.24 Mechanical Execution of Work

Equipment and cabling must be installed in a neat and workman-like manner. Exposed cables and conductors must be supported by the structural components of the building so that the cable won't be

damaged by normal building use. Such cables must be supported by straps, staples, hangers, cable ties, or similar fittings designed and installed in a manner that won't damage the cable. Figure 725–10

Figure 725–10

Author's Comment:

■ Raceways and cables can be supported by independent support wires attached to the suspended ceiling in accordance with 300.11(A) [725.46 and 725.143]. Figure 725–11

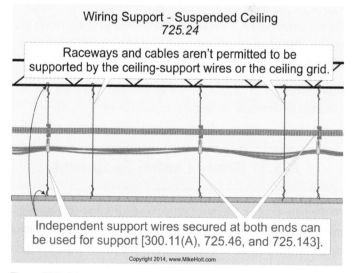

Figure 725–11

Cables installed through or parallel to framing members or furring strips must be protected, where they're likely to be penetrated by nails or screws, by installing the wiring method so it isn't less than 1¼ in. from the nearest edge of the framing member or furring strips, or by protecting them with a ¹⁄₁₆ in. thick steel plate or equivalent [300.4(D)]. Figure 725–12

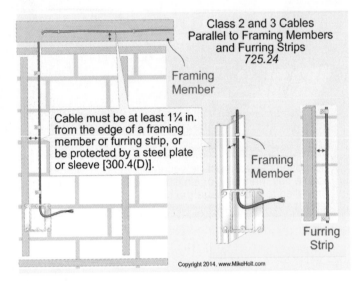

Figure 725–12

725.25 Abandoned Cable

To limit the spread of fire or products of combustion within a building, the accessible portion of cable that isn't terminated at equipment and not identified for future use with a tag must be removed [725.2]. Figure 725–13

Cables identified for future use must be identified with a tag that can withstand the environment involved. Figure 725–14

725.31 Safety-Control Equipment

(A) Remote-Control Circuits. Circuits used for safety-control equipment must be classified as Class 1 if the failure of the remote-control circuit or equipment introduces a direct fire or life hazard. Figure 725–15

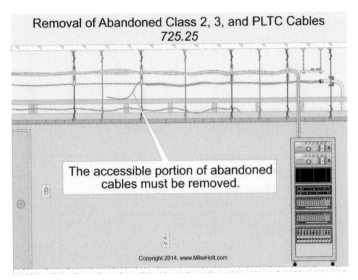

Figure 725–13

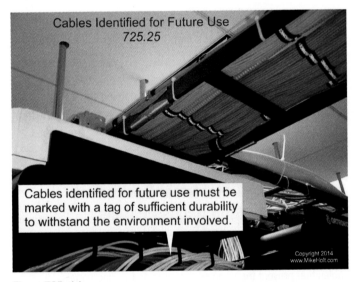

Figure 725–14

Room thermostats, water-temperature regulating devices, and similar controls used in conjunction with electrically controlled household heating and air-conditioning, aren't considered safety-control equipment.

(B) Physical Protection. If damage to remote-control circuits of safety-control equipment would introduce a hazard [725.31(A)], conductors must be installed in rigid metal conduit, intermediate metal conduit, PVC conduit, electrical metallic tubing, Type MI cable, Type MC cable, or be otherwise suitably protected from physical damage.

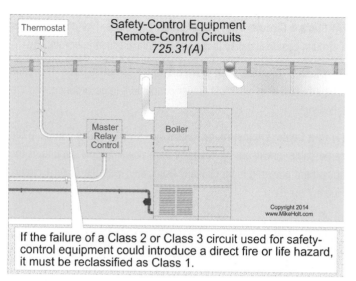

Figure 725–15

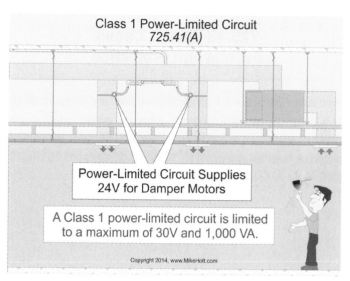

Figure 725–16

725.35 Circuit Requirements

(1) Class 1 circuits must comply with Parts I and II of Article 725.

(2) Class 2 and Class 3 circuits must comply with Parts I and III of Article 725.

Part II. Class 1 Circuit Requirements

725.41 Class 1 Circuit Classifications and Power-Supply Requirements

(A) Class 1 Power-Limited Circuits. Class 1 power-limited circuits must be supplied from a power supply that limits the output to 30V with no more than 1,000 VA. Figure 725–16

Author's Comment:

- Class 1 power-limited circuits aren't that common. They're used when the voltage must be less than 30V (safe from electric shock in dry locations), and where the power demands exceed the 100 VA energy limitations of Class 2 or Class 3 circuits, such as for motorized loads like remote-controlled window blinds [Chapter 9, Table 11(A)].

(B) Class 1 Remote-Control and Signaling Circuits. Class 1 remote-control and signaling circuits must not operate at more than 600V, and the power output of the power supply isn't required to be limited. Figure 725–17

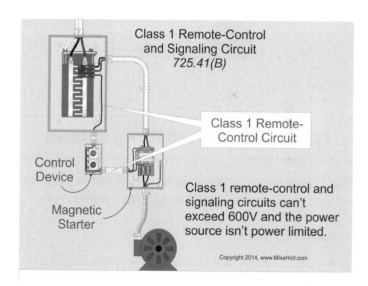

Figure 725–17

725.43 Class 1 Circuit Overcurrent Protection

Overcurrent protection for conductors 14 AWG and larger must be in accordance with the conductor ampacity, without applying the ampacity adjustment or correction factors of 310.15, and overcurrent protection must not exceed 7A for 18 AWG conductors and 10A for 16 AWG. Figure 725–18

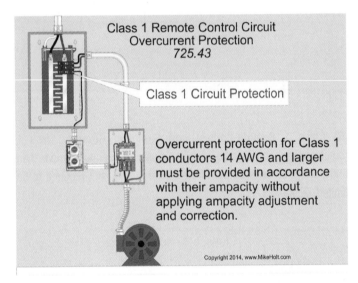

Figure 725–18

725.46 Class 1 Circuit Wiring Methods

Class 1 circuits must be installed in accordance with Part I of Article 300, and Class 1 wiring must be installed using Chapter 3 wiring methods.

Author's Comment:

- Class 1 circuits must be installed in a suitable Chapter 3 wiring method and splices must be contained in enclosures [300.15].

725.48 Conductors of Different Circuits in Same Cable, Cable Tray, Enclosure, or Raceway

Class 1 circuits can be installed with other circuits as follows:

(A) Class 1 Circuits with Other Class 1 Circuits. Two or more Class 1 circuits can be installed in the same cable, enclosure, or raceway.

(B) Class 1 Circuits with Power-Supply Circuits. Class 1 circuits are permitted with electrical power conductors in accordance with the following:

(1) In a Cable, Enclosure, or Raceway. Class 1 circuits can be in the same cable, enclosure, or raceway with power-supply circuits, if the equipment powered is functionally associated with the Class 1 circuit. Figure 725–19

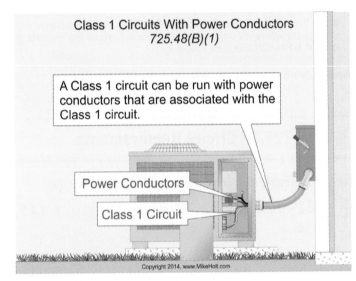

Figure 725–19

(4) In Cable Trays. Class 1 circuits not functionally associated with power conductors:

(1) Must be separated by a solid fixed barrier, or

(2) Be installed in Type AC, Type MC, Type MI, or Type TC cables.

725.49 Class 1 Circuit Conductors

(A) Size and Use. Conductors of sizes 18 AWG and 16 AWG installed in a raceway, enclosure, or listed cable are permitted if they don't supply a load that exceeds the ampacities given in 402.5. Conductors 14 AWG and larger must not supply loads greater than the ampacities given in 310.15.

(B) Insulation. Class 1 circuit conductors must have at least a 600V insulation rating. Conductors larger than 16 AWG must comply with Article 310.

725.51 Number of Conductors in a Raceway

(A) Class 1 Circuit Conductors. Raceways must be large enough to permit the installation and removal of conductors without damaging conductor insulation as limited by 300.17.

Author's Comment:

- When all conductors in a raceway are the same size and insulation, the number of conductors permitted can be found in Annex C for the raceway type.

Question: How many 18 TFFN fixture wires can be installed in trade size ½ electrical metallic tubing? Figure 725–20

(a) 22   (b) 26   (c) 30   (d) 40

Answer: (a) 22 [Annex C, Table C.1]

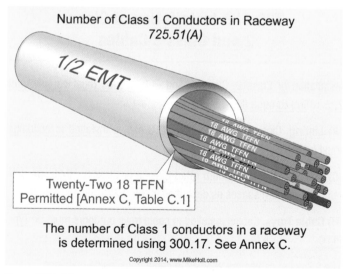

Number of Class 1 Conductors in Raceway
725.51(A)

Twenty-Two 18 TFFN
Permitted [Annex C, Table C.1]

The number of Class 1 conductors in a raceway is determined using 300.17. See Annex C.

Copyright 2014, www.MikeHolt.com

Figure 725–20

The ampacity adjustment factors of Table 310.15(B)(3)(a) only apply to Class 1 circuit conductors carrying continuous loads in excess of 10 percent of the ampacity of each conductor.

Part III. Class 2 and Class 3 Circuit Requirements

725.121 Power Sources for Class 2 and Class 3 Circuits

(A) Power Source. The power supply for a Class 2 or a Class 3 circuit must be:

(1) A listed Class 2 or Class 3 transformer. Figure 725–21

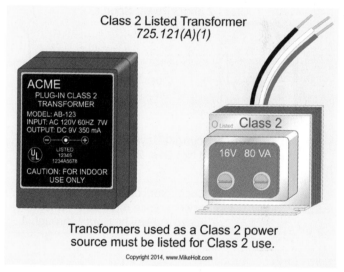

Class 2 Listed Transformer
725.121(A)(1)

ACME
PLUG-IN CLASS 2
TRANSFORMER
MODEL: AB-123
INPUT: AC 120V 60HZ 7W
OUTPUT: DC 9V 350 mA
LISTED
12345
1234A5678
CAUTION: FOR INDOOR
USE ONLY

Class 2
16V 80 VA

Transformers used as a Class 2 power source must be listed for Class 2 use.

Copyright 2014, www.MikeHolt.com

Figure 725–21

(2) A listed Class 2 or Class 3 power supply. See Figure 725–21.

(3) Equipment listed as a Class 2 or Class 3 power source.

Ex 2: Where each circuit has an energy level at or below the limits established in Chapter 9, Table 11(A) and Table 11(B), the equipment isn't required to be listed as a Class 2 or Class 3 power transformer, power supply, or power source.

(4) Listed information technology equipment.

(5) A dry cell battery rated 30V or less for a Class 2 circuit.

725.124 Equipment Marking

Equipment supplying Class 2 or Class 3 circuits must be marked to indicate each circuit that's a Class 2 or Class 3 circuit.

725.127 Wiring Methods on Supply Side of the Class 2 or Class 3 Power Source

Conductors and equipment on the supply side of the Class 2 or Class 3 power supply must be installed in accordance with Chapters 1 through 4. Figure 725–22

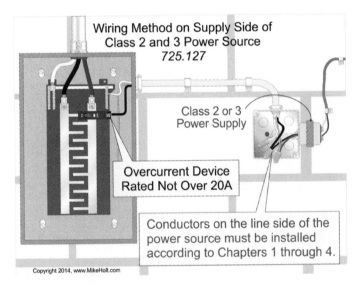

Figure 725–22

725.130 Wiring Methods on Load Side of the Class 2 or Class 3 Power Source

(A) Class 1 Wiring Methods. Class 2 or Class 3 circuits can use a Chapter 3 wiring method [725.46].

Ex 2: Class 2 and Class 3 circuits can be reclassified as a Class 1 circuit if the Class 2 and Class 3 equipment markings required by 725.124 are eliminated and the entire circuit is installed using a Chapter 3 wiring method in accordance with Part II of Article 725 for Class 1 circuits. Figure 725–23

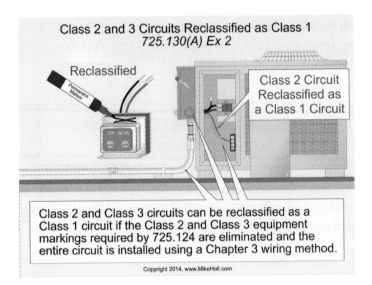

Figure 725–23

Note: Class 2 and Class 3 circuits reclassified and installed as Class 1 circuits are no longer Class 2 or Class 3 circuits, regardless of their continued connection to a Class 2 or Class 3 power source.

(B) Class 2 and Class 3 Wiring Methods. Class 2 and Class 3 circuit conductors must be of the type listed and marked in accordance with 725.179, and they must be installed in accordance with 725.133 and 725.154.

725.135 Installation of Class 2 and Class 3 Cables

Installation of Class 2, Class 3, and PLTC cables must comply with 725.135(A) through (M).

(A) Listing. Class 2, Class 3, and PLTC cables installed in buildings must be listed.

(C) Plenum Spaces. Plenum rated Class 2 or Class 3 cables are permitted in plenum spaces as described in 300.22(C): Figure 725–24

(H) Cable Trays. Cables installed in cable trays outdoors must be Type PLTC.

The following cables are allowed in cable trays inside buildings:

(1) Types CM, CL2P, CL3P, CL2R, CL3R, CL2, CL3, and PLTC cables

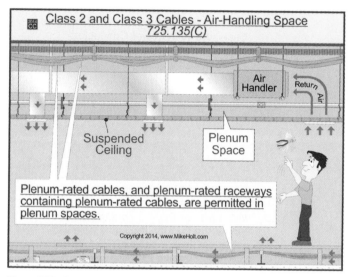

Figure 725–24

(2) Types CL2P, CL3P, CL2R, CL3R, CL2, CL3, and PLTC cables installed in:

a. Plenum communications raceways

b. Riser communications raceways

c. General-purpose communications raceways

(K) Other Building Locations. The following cables are allowed in building locations other than the locations covered in 725.135(B) through (I):

(1) Types CL2P, CL3P, CL2R, CL3R, CL2, CL3 and PLTC cables

(2) A maximum of 10 ft of exposed Type CL2X in nonconcealed spaces

(3) A maximum of 10 ft of exposed Type CL3X in nonconcealed spaces

(4) Types CL2P, CL3P, CL2R, CL3R, CL2, CL3, and PLTC cables installed in:

a. Plenum communications raceways

b. Plenum cable routing assemblies

c. Riser communications raceways

d. Riser cable routing assemblies

e. General-purpose communications raceways

f. General-purpose cable routing assemblies

(5) Types CL2P, CL3P, CL2R, CL3R, CL2, CL3, CL2X, CL3X, and PLTC cables installed in raceways recognized in Chapter 3

(6) Type CMUC undercarpet communications cables installed under carpet

(M) One- and Two-Family dwellings. The following cables are allowed in one- and two-family dwellings in locations other than the locations covered in 725.135 (B) through (I):

(1) Types CL2P, CL3P, CL2R, CL3R, CL2, CL3, and PLTC cables

(2) Type CL2X less than ¼ in. in diameter

(3) Type CL3X less than ¼ in. in diameter

(4) Communications cables and Types CL2P, CL3P, CL2R, CL3R, CL2, CL3, and PLTC cables installed in:

a Plenum communications raceways

b. Plenum cable routing assemblies

c. Riser communications raceways

d. Riser cable routing assemblies

e. General-purpose communications raceways

f. General-purpose cable routing assemblies

(5) Types CL2P, CL3P, CL2R, CL3R, CL2, CL3, CL2X, CL3X, and PLTC cables installed in raceways recognized in Chapter 3

(6) Type CMUC undercarpet communications cables installed under carpet

725.136 Separation from Power Conductors

(A) Enclosures, Raceways, or Cables. Class 2 and Class 3 circuit conductors must not be placed in any enclosure, raceway, or cable with conductors of electric light, power, and Class 1 circuits, except as permitted in (B) through (J). Figure 725–25, Figure 725–26, and Figure 725–27

(B) Separated by Barriers. Class 2 and Class 3 circuit conductors must not be placed in any enclosure with conductors of electric power or Class 1 conductors unless separated by a barrier. Figure 725–28 and Figure 725–29

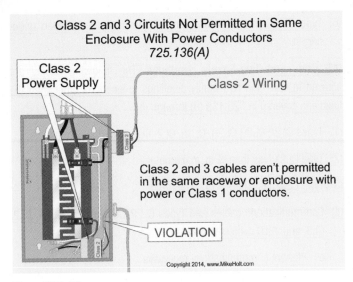

Figure 725–25

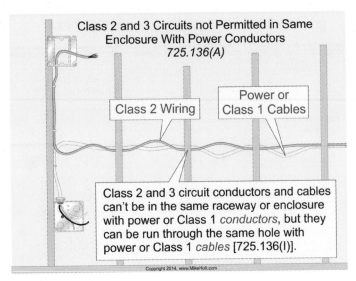

Figure 725–27

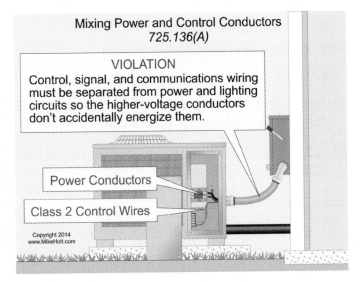

Figure 725–26

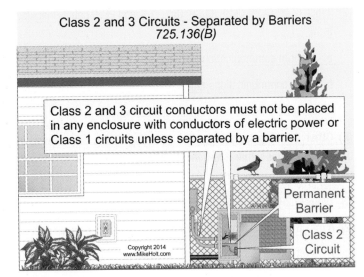

Figure 725–28

Author's Comment:

- Separation is required to prevent a fire or shock hazard that can occur from a short between the Class 2 or Class 3 circuit and the higher-voltage circuits.

(D) Within Enclosures. Class 2 and Class 3 conductors can be mixed with electric light, power, and Class 1 conductors in enclosures if these other conductors are introduced solely for connection to the same equipment as the Class 2 or Class 3 circuits, and:

(1) A minimum ¼ in. separation is maintained from the Class 2 or Class 3 conductors.

(I) Other Applications. Class 2 and Class 3 circuit conductors must be separated by not less than 2 in. from insulated conductors of electric light, power, and Class 1 circuits, unless:

(1) Electrical power and Class 1 circuit conductors are in a raceway or metal-sheathed or nonmetallic-sheathed cable, or the Class 2 and Class 3 circuit conductors are in a raceway or metal-sheathed or nonmetallic-sheathed cable. Figure 725–30

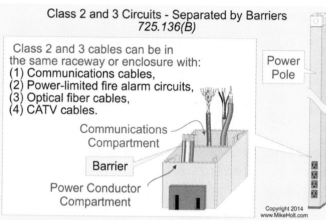

Class 2 and 3 Circuits - Separated by Barriers
725.136(B)

Class 2 and 3 cables can be in the same raceway or enclosure with:
(1) Communications cables,
(2) Power-limited fire alarm circuits,
(3) Optical fiber cables,
(4) CATV cables.

Communications Compartment

Barrier

Power Conductor Compartment

Power Pole

Copyright 2014
www.MikeHolt.com

Class 2 and Class 3 circuit conductors must not be placed in any enclosure with conductors of electric power or Class 1 unless separated by a barrier.

Figure 725–29

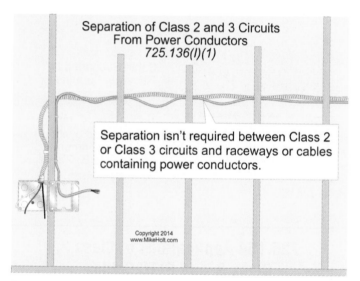

Separation of Class 2 and 3 Circuits
From Power Conductors
725.136(I)(1)

Separation isn't required between Class 2 or Class 3 circuits and raceways or cables containing power conductors.

Copyright 2014
www.MikeHolt.com

Figure 725–30

725.139 Conductors of Different Circuits in Same Cable, Enclosure, Cable Tray, Raceway, or Cable Routing Assembly

(A) Class 2 Conductors. Class 2 circuit conductors can be in the same cable, cable routing assembly, enclosure, or raceway with other Class 2 circuit conductors.

(B) Class 3 Conductors. Class 3 circuit conductors can be in the same cable, cable routing assembly, enclosure, or raceway with other Class 3 circuit conductors.

(C) Class 2 Conductors with Class 3 Conductors. Class 2 conductors are permitted within the same cable, cable routing assembly, enclosure, or raceway with Class 3 circuit conductors, provided insulation of the Class 2 circuit conductors is at least that required for Class 3 circuits.

Author's Comment:

■ Listed Class 2 cables have an insulation rating of at least 150V, whereas listed Class 3 cables are rated at least 300V [725.179(G)].

(D) Class 2 and Class 3 Circuits with Communications Circuits.

(1) Classified as Communications Circuits. Class 2 and Class 3 circuit conductors can be within the same cables with communications circuits in listed communications cables in which case they're classified as communications circuits and must be installed in accordance with Article 800.

Author's Comment:

■ A common application of this requirement is when a single communications cable is used for both voice communications and data.

■ Listed Class 2 cables have an insulation rating of at least 150V insulation [725.179(G)], whereas listed communications cables have a voltage rating of at least 300V [800.179].

(E) Class 2 or Class 3 Cables with Other Cables. Class 2 or Class 3 jacketed cables can be in the same enclosure, cable tray, raceway, or cable routing assembly as jacketed cables of any of the following: Figure 725–31

(1) Power-limited fire alarm circuits in compliance with Parts I and III of Article 760.

(2) Nonconductive and conductive optical fiber cables in compliance with Parts I and IV of Article 770.

(3) Communications circuits in compliance with Parts I and IV of Article 800.

(4) Coaxial cables in compliance with Parts I and IV of Article 820.

(F) Class 2 or Class 3 Circuits with Audio System Circuits. Audio output circuits [640.9(C)] using Class 2 or Class 3 wiring methods in compliance with 725.136 and 725.154 aren't permitted in any cable routing assembly, raceway, or cable with Class 2 or Class 3 conductors or cables.

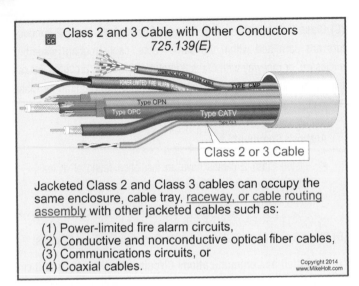

Jacketed Class 2 and Class 3 cables can occupy the same enclosure, cable tray, raceway, or cable routing assembly with other jacketed cables such as:

(1) Power-limited fire alarm circuits,
(2) Conductive and nonconductive optical fiber cables,
(3) Communications circuits, or
(4) Coaxial cables.

Figure 725–31

Author's Comment:

■ The concern is that a fault from audio amplifier circuits to a Class 2 and Class 3 circuit has the potential of creating a hazard by disrupting the operation of alarm systems and remote-control circuits for safety-control equipment.

725.143 Support

Class 2 or Class 3 cables aren't permitted to be strapped, taped, or attached to the exterior of any raceway as a means of support. Figure 725–32

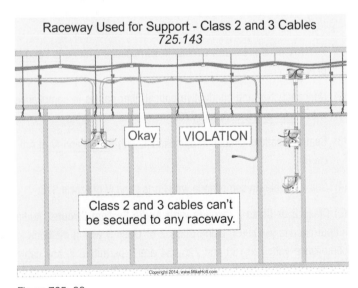

Figure 725–32

Author's Comment:

■ Exposed cables must be supported by the structural components of the building so the cable won't be damaged by normal building use, and cables must be secured by straps, staples, hangers, or similar fittings designed and installed in a manner that won't damage the cable [725.24].

Class 2 control cables can be supported by the raceway that supplies power to the equipment controlled by the Class 2 cable [300.11(B)(2)]. Figure 725–33

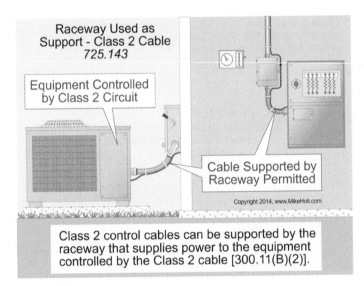

Figure 725–33

725.154 Applications of Class 2, Class 3, and PLTC Cables

Class 2, Class 3, and PLTC cables must comply with the requirements of (A) through (C), as indicated in Table 725.154.

(A) Class 2 and Class 3 Cable Substitutions. *NEC* Figure 725.154(A) Cable Substitution Hierarchy and *NEC* Table 725.154 describe where Class 2 and Class 3 cables can be used. Figure 725–34

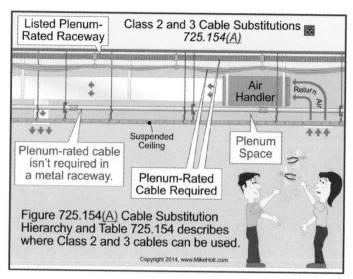

Figure 725–34

Part IV. Listing Requirements

725.179 Listing and Marking of Class 2 and Class 3 Cables

Class 2, Class 3 cables, nonmetallic signaling raceways, and cable routing assemblies installed within buildings must be listed as being resistant to the spread of fire and other criteria in accordance with 725.179(A) through (J) and shall be marked in accordance with 725.179(K). Figure 725–35

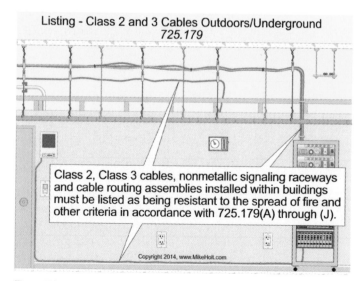

Figure 725–35

(A) Types CL2P and CL3P. Types CL2P and CL3P plenum cable are listed as being suitable for use in plenum space and listed as having adequate fire-resistance and low-smoke producing characteristics. Figure 725–36

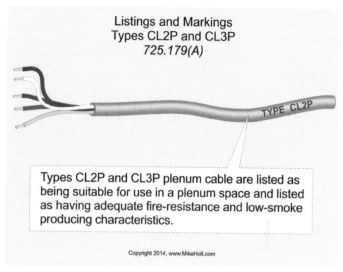

Figure 725–36

(G) Cable Voltage Rating. Class 2 cables must have a voltage rating not less than 150V, and Class 3 cables must have a voltage rating not less than 300V.

(K) Marking. Voltage ratings aren't permitted to be marked on the cable.

> Note: Voltage markings on cables may suggest that the cables are suitable for Class 1 or electric power and light applications, which they aren't.

ARTICLE 725 PRACTICE QUESTIONS

Please use the 2014 *Code* book to answer the following questions.

1. Class 2 and Class 3 cable not terminated at equipment and not identified for future use with a tag is considered abandoned.

   (a) True
   (b) False

2. Due to its power limitations, a Class 2 circuit is considered safe from a fire initiation standpoint and provides acceptable protection from electric shock.

   (a) True
   (b) False

3. Since Class 3 control circuits permit higher allowable levels of voltage and current than Class 2 control circuits, additional _____ are specified to provide protection against the electric shock hazard.

   (a) circuits
   (b) safeguards
   (c) conditions
   (d) requirements

4. Class 1, 2, and 3 circuits installed through fire-resistant-rated walls, partitions, floors, or ceilings must be firestopped to limit the possible spread of fire or products of combustion.

   (a) True
   (b) False

5. If remote-control, signaling, and power-limited circuits are installed in a raceway that is subjected to different temperatures, and where condensation is known to be a problem, the raceway must be filled with a material approved by the authority having jurisdiction that will prevent the circulation of warm air to a colder section of the raceway. An explosionproof seal _____.

   (a) is required for this purpose
   (b) has been proven effective for this purpose
   (c) isn't required for this purpose
   (d) is the only method of doing this

6. When a raceway is used for the support or protection of cables for remote-control, signaling, and power-limited circuits, a bushing to reduce the potential for abrasion must be placed at the location the cables enter the raceway.

   (a) True
   (b) False

7. Access to electrical equipment shall not be denied by an accumulation of remote-control, signaling, or power-limited wire and cables that prevent removal of panels, including suspended-ceiling panels.

   (a) True
   (b) False

8. Class 2 and Class 3 circuits installed _____ on the surface of ceilings and walls shall be supported by the building structure in such a manner that the cable will not be damaged by normal building use.

    (a) exposed
    (b) concealed
    (c) hidden
    (d) a and b

9. Exposed Class 2 and Class 3 cables shall be supported by straps, staples, hangers, or similar fittings designed and installed so as not to damage the cable.

    (a) True
    (b) False

10. Accessible portions of abandoned Class 2 and Class 3 cables shall be removed.

    (a) True
    (b) False

11. Class 2 cables identified for future use shall be marked with a tag of sufficient durability to withstand _____.

    (a) moisture
    (b) humidity
    (c) the environment involved
    (d) none of these

12. Remote-control circuits to safety-control equipment shall be classified as _____ if the failure of the equipment to operate introduces a direct fire or life hazard.

    (a) Class 1
    (b) Class 2
    (c) Class 3
    (d) Class I, Division 1

13. Power-supply conductors and Class 1 circuit conductors can occupy the same cable, enclosure, or raceway _____.

    (a) only where both are functionally associated with the equipment powered
    (b) where the circuits involved are not a mixture of ac and dc
    (c) under no circumstances
    (d) none of these

14. The power source for a Class 2 circuit shall be _____.

    (a) a listed Class 2 transformer
    (b) a listed Class 2 power supply
    (c) other listed equipment marked to identify the Class 2 power source
    (d) any of these

15. Equipment supplying Class 2 or Class 3 circuits shall be durably marked where plainly visible to indicate _____.

    (a) each circuit that is a Class 2 or Class 3 circuit
    (b) the circuit VA rating
    (c) the size of conductors serving each circuit
    (d) all of these

16. Cables and conductors of Class 2 and Class 3 circuits _____ be placed with conductors of electric light, power, Class 1, nonpower-limited fire alarm circuits, and medium power network-powered broadband communications circuits.

    (a) shall be permitted to
    (b) shall not
    (c) shall
    (d) none of these

17. Conductors of Class 2 and Class 3 circuits shall not be placed in any enclosure, raceway, cable, or similar fittings with conductors of Class 1 or electric light or power conductors, unless _____.

    (a) insulated for the maximum voltage present
    (b) totally comprised of aluminum conductors
    (c) separated by a barrier
    (d) all of these

18. Audio system circuits using Class 2 or Class 3 wiring methods are not permitted in the same cable, raceway, or cable routing assembly with _____.

    (a) other audio system circuits
    (b) Class 2 conductors or cables
    (c) Class 3 conductors or cables
    (d) b or c

19. Raceways shall not be used as a means of support for Class 2 or Class 3 cables.

    (a) True
    (b) False

FIRE ALARM SYSTEMS

Introduction to Article 760—Fire Alarm Systems

Article 760 covers the installation of wiring and equipment for fire alarm systems, including circuits controlled and powered by the fire alarm. These include fire detection and alarm notification, guard's tour, sprinkler waterflow, and sprinkler supervisory systems. NFPA 72, *National Fire Alarm Code* provides other fire alarm system requirements.

Part I. General

760.1 Scope

Article 760 covers the installation of wiring and equipment for fire alarm systems, including circuits controlled and powered by the fire alarm system. Figure 760–1

Fire Alarm Systems
760.1

FIRE FIRE

PULL DOWN
FIRE
ALARM

Article 760 covers the installation of wiring and equipment for fire alarm systems.

Copyright 2014, www.MikeHolt.com

Figure 760–1

Author's Comment:

■ Residential smoke alarm systems, including interconnecting wiring, aren't covered by Article 760, because they aren't powered by a fire alarm system as defined in NFPA 72.

Note 1: Fire alarm systems include fire detection and alarm notification, guard's tour, sprinkler waterflow, and sprinkler supervisory systems. Other circuits that might be controlled or powered by the fire alarm system include elevator capture, elevator shutdown, door release, smoke doors and damper control, fire doors and damper control, and fan shutdown.

NFPA 72, *National Fire Alarm and Signaling Code,* provides the requirements for the selection, installation, performance, use, testing, and maintenance of fire alarm systems.

Author's Comment:

■ Building control circuits associated with the fire alarm system, such as elevator capture and fan shutdown, must comply with Article 725 [760.3(E)]. Article 760 applies if these components are powered and directly controlled by the fire alarm system.

■ NFPA 101—*Life Safety Code* or the local building code specifies when and where a fire alarm system is required.

760.2 Definitions

Abandoned Fire Alarm Cable. A cable that isn't terminated to equipment and not identified for future use with a tag.

Author's Comment:

- Section 760.25 requires the accessible portion of abandoned cables to be removed.

Fire Alarm Circuit. The portion of the wiring system and connected equipment powered and controlled by the fire alarm system. Fire alarm circuits are classified as either nonpower-limited or power-limited.

Nonpower-Limited Fire Alarm Circuit. A nonpower-limited fire alarm circuit can operate at up to 600V, and the power output isn't limited [760.41 and 760.43]. Figure 760–2

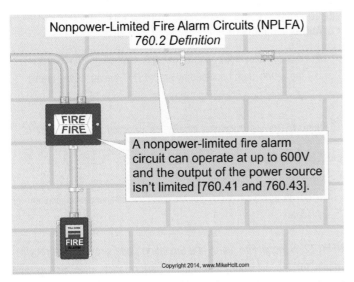

Nonpower-Limited Fire Alarm Circuits (NPLFA)
760.2 Definition

FIRE
FIRE

A nonpower-limited fire alarm circuit can operate at up to 600V and the output of the power source isn't limited [760.41 and 760.43].

FIRE
ALARM

Copyright 2014, www.MikeHolt.com

Figure 760–2

Power-Limited Fire Alarm Circuit. A power-limited fire alarm circuit must have the voltage and power limited by a listed power supply that complies with 760.121 as follows: Figure 760–3

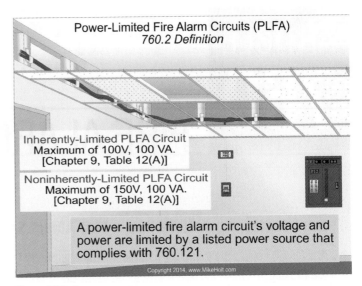

Power-Limited Fire Alarm Circuits (PLFA)
760.2 Definition

Inherently-Limited PLFA Circuit
Maximum of 100V, 100 VA.
[Chapter 9, Table 12(A)]

Noninherently-Limited PLFA Circuit
Maximum of 150V, 100 VA.
[Chapter 9, Table 12(A)]

A power-limited fire alarm circuit's voltage and power are limited by a listed power source that complies with 760.121.

Copyright 2014, www.MikeHolt.com

Figure 760–3

Inherently Limited (ac) [Chapter 9, Table 12(A)]	
Voltage	Power
0V to 20V	5.00 x V
21V to 100V	100 VA

Not Inherently Limited [Chapter 9, Table 12(A)]		
Overcurrent Voltage	Power	Protection
0V to 20V	5.00 x V	5A
21V to 100V	100 VA	100/V
101V to 150V	100 VA	1A

Author's Comment:

- Inherently limited power supplies are designed to burn out if overloaded.

760.3 Other Articles

Only those sections of Article 300 specifically referenced in this article apply to fire alarm systems, and fire alarm circuits and equipment must comply with (A) through (G) as follows:

(A) Spread of Fire or Products of Combustion. Fire alarm circuits installed through fire-resistant-rated walls, partitions, floors, or ceilings must be firestopped to limit the possible spread of fire or products of combustion in accordance with the instructions supplied by the manufacturer for the specific type of cable and construction material (drywall, brick, and so forth) [300.21]. Figure 760–4

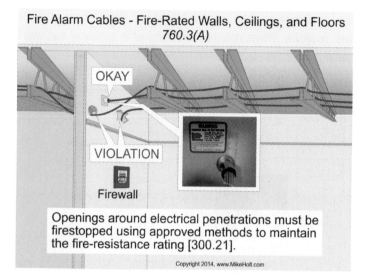

Fire Alarm Cables - Fire-Rated Walls, Ceilings, and Floors
760.3(A)

OKAY

VIOLATION

Firewall

Openings around electrical penetrations must be firestopped using approved methods to maintain the fire-resistance rating [300.21].

Copyright 2014, www.MikeHolt.com

Figure 760–4

(D) Corrosive, Damp, or Wet Locations. Fire alarm circuits installed in corrosive, damp, or wet locations must be identified for use in the operating environment [110.11], must be of materials suitable for the environment in which they're to be installed, and must be of a type suitable for the application [300.5(B), 300.6, 300.9, and 310.10(G)].

(E) Building Control Circuits. Class 1, 2, and 3 circuits used for building controls (elevator capture, fan shutdown, and so on), associated with the fire alarm system, but not controlled and powered by the fire alarm system, must be installed in accordance with Article 725 [760.1].

(F) Optical Fiber Cables. Optical fiber cables utilized for fire alarm circuits must be installed in accordance with Article 770.

(H) Raceways or Sleeves Exposed to Different Temperatures. If a raceway or sleeve is subjected to different temperatures, and where condensation is known to be a problem, the raceway or sleeve must be filled with a material approved by the authority having jurisdiction that will prevent the circulation of warm air to a colder section of the raceway. An explosionproof seal isn't required for this purpose [300.7(A)]. Figure 760–5

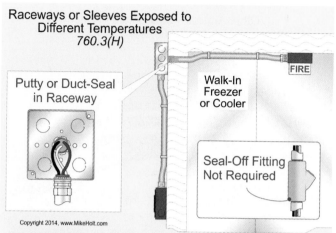

Raceways or Sleeves Exposed to
Different Temperatures
760.3(H)

Putty or Duct-Seal
in Raceway

FIRE

Walk-In
Freezer
or Cooler

Seal-Off Fitting
Not Required

Copyright 2014, www.MikeHolt.com

Raceways must be sealed to prevent the circulation of warm air to a colder section of the raceway or sleeve [300.7(A)].

Figure 760–5

(J) Number and Size of Conductors in a Raceway. Raceways must be large enough to permit the installation and removal of conductors without damaging conductor insulation [300.17].

Author's Comment:

■ When all conductors in a raceway are the same size and insulation, the number of conductors permitted can be found in Annex C for the raceway type.

Question: How many 18 TFFN fixture wires can be installed in trade size ½ electrical metallic tubing? Figure 760–6

(a) 22   (b) 26   (c) 30   (d) 40

Answer: (a) 22 conductors [Annex C, Table C.1]

(K) Bushing. When a raceway is used for the support or protection of cables, a bushing to reduce the potential for abrasion must be placed at the location where the cables enter the raceway in accordance with 300.15(C). Figure 760–7

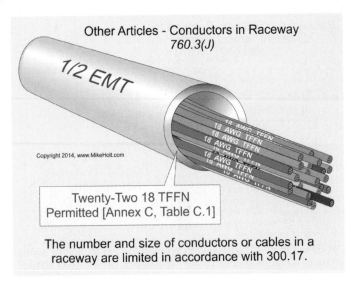

Figure 760-6

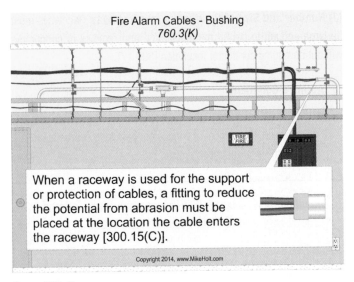

Figure 760-7

760.21 Access to Electrical Equipment Behind Panels Designed to Allow Access

Access to equipment must not be prohibited by an accumulation of cables that prevent the removal of suspended-ceiling panels.

Author's Comment:

■ Cables must be located so that the suspended-ceiling panels can be moved to provide access to electrical equipment.

760.24 Mechanical Execution of Work

(A) General. Equipment and cabling must be installed in a neat and workmanlike manner.

Exposed cables must be supported by the structural components of the building so that the cable won't be damaged by normal building use. Cables must be supported by straps, staples, hangers, cable ties, or similar fittings designed and installed in a manner that won't damage the cable. Figure 760-8

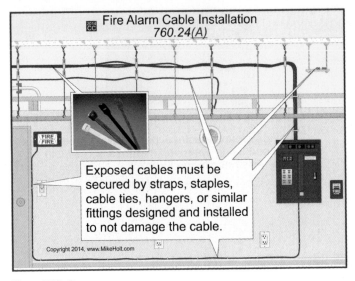

Figure 760-8

Author's Comment:

■ Raceways and cables above a suspended ceiling must be supported by independent support wires attached to the suspended ceiling [300.11(A), 760.46, and 760.130]. Figure 760-9

Cables installed through or parallel to framing members or furring strips must be protected where they're likely to be penetrated by nails or screws, by installing the wiring method so it isn't less than 1¼ in. from the nearest edge of the framing member or furring strips, or by protecting them with a ¹⁄₁₆ in. thick steel plate or the equivalent [300.4(D)]. Figure 760-10

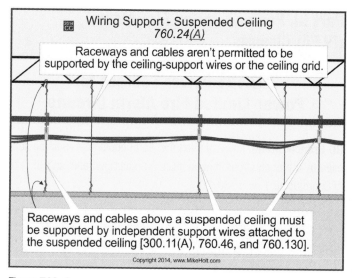

Figure 760–9

Figure 760–11

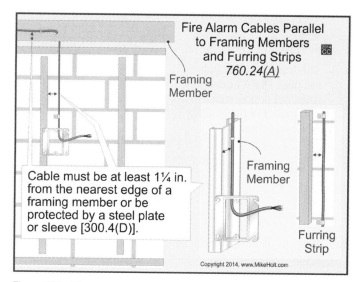

Figure 760–10

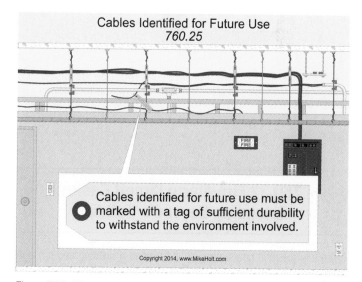

Figure 760–12

760.25 Abandoned Cable

To limit the spread of fire or products of combustion within a building, the accessible portion of cable that isn't terminated at equipment and not identified for future use with a tag must be removed [760.2]. Figure 760–11

Cables identified for future use must be with a tag that can withstand the environment involved. Figure 760–12

Author's Comment:

■ Cables installed in concealed raceways aren't considered "accessible"; therefore, they're not required to be removed.

760.30 Fire Alarm Circuit Identification

Fire alarm circuits must be identified at terminal and junction locations. The identification must be in such a manner that will help to prevent unintentional signals on the fire alarm system circuits during testing and servicing of other systems. Figure 760–13

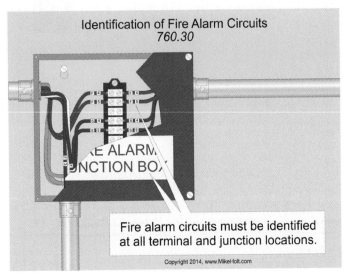

Identification of Fire Alarm Circuits
760.30

Fire alarm circuits must be identified at all terminal and junction locations.

Copyright 2014, www.MikeHolt.com

Figure 760–13

760.32 Fire Alarm Circuit Cables Extending Beyond a Building

If fire alarm circuit conductors extend beyond a building and run out-doors, they must be installed in accordance with Parts II, III, and IV of Article 800, and they must also be installed in accordance with Part I of Article 300.

760.35 Fire Alarm Circuit Requirements

(A) Nonpower-Limited Fire Alarm Circuits. Nonpower-limited fire alarm (NPLFA) circuits must comply with Parts I and II of this article.

(B) Power-Limited Fire Alarm Circuits. Power-limited fire alarm (PLFA) circuits must comply with Parts I and III of this article.

Part III. Power-Limited Fire Alarm (PLFA) Circuits

760.121 Power Sources for Power-Limited Fire Alarm Circuits

(B) Branch Circuit. Power-limited fire alarm equipment must be supplied by a branch circuit that supplies no other load and isn't GFCI or AFCI protected. Figure 760–14

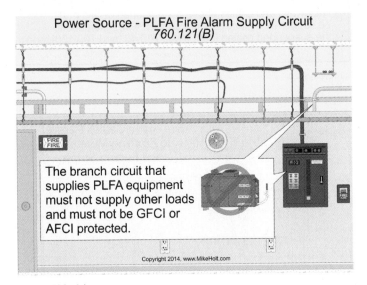

Power Source - PLFA Fire Alarm Supply Circuit
760.121(B)

FIRE FIRE

The branch circuit that supplies PLFA equipment must not supply other loads and must not be GFCI or AFCI protected.

Copyright 2014, www.MikeHolt.com

Figure 760–14

The location of the branch-circuit overcurrent device for the power-limited fire alarm equipment must be permanently identified at the fire alarm control unit. Figure 760–15

The branch-circuit overcurrent device must be identified in red, accessible only to qualified personnel, and identified as "FIRE ALARM CIRCUIT." The red identification must not damage the overcurrent protective device or obscure any manufacturer's markings. Figure 760–16

760.124 Equipment Marking

Fire alarm equipment supplying power-limited fire alarm cable circuits must be durably marked to indicate each circuit that's a power-limited fire alarm circuit.

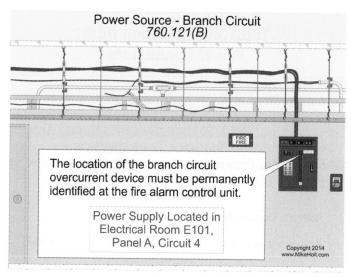

Figure 760–15

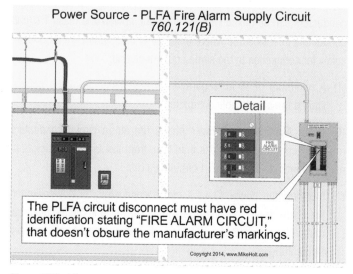

Figure 760–16

Author's Comment:

■ Fire alarm circuits must be marked at terminal and junction locations [760.30].

760.130 Wiring Methods on Load Side of Power-Limited Fire Alarm Power Source

(B) PLFA Wiring Methods and Materials. Power-limited fire alarm conductors and cables described in 760.179 must be installed as detailed in (1), (2), or (3) of this section and 300.7.

(1) Exposed or Fished in Concealed Spaces. Cable splices or terminations must be made in listed fittings, boxes, enclosures, fire alarm devices, or utilization equipment. Figure 760–17

Figure 760–17

Power-limited fire alarm cable installed exposed must be adequately supported and protected against physical damage.

Author's Comment:

■ Exposed cables must be supported by the structural components of the building so the cable won't be damaged by normal building use. Cables must be secured by straps, staples, hangers, or similar fittings designed and installed in a manner that won't damage the cable. Cables installed through or parallel to framing members or furring strips must be protected where they're likely to be penetrated by nails or screws, by installing the wiring method so it isn't less than 1¼ in. from the nearest edge of the framing member or furring strips, or it must be protected by a ⅟₁₆ in. thick steel plate or the equivalent [760.24(A)].

760.135 Installation of PLFA Cables in Buildings

Installation of power-limited fire alarm cables in buildings must comply with 760.135(A) through (J).

(A) Listing. PLFA cables installed in buildings must be listed.

(C) Plenum Spaces. Plenum rated FPLP cables are permitted in plenum spaces as described in 300.22(C). Figure 760–18

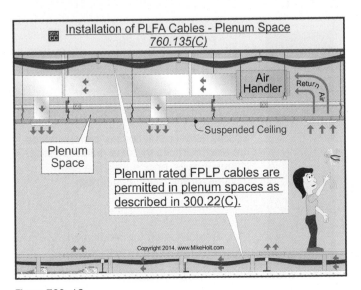

Figure 760–18

(H) Other Building Locations. The following cables are permitted to be installed in building locations other than the locations covered in 770.113(B) through (H):

(1) Types FPLP, FPLR, and FPL cables

(2) Types FPLP, FPLR, and FPL cables installed in:

   a. Plenum communications raceways

   b. Plenum cable routing assemblies

   c. Riser communications raceways

   d. Riser cable routing assemblies

   e. General-purpose communications raceways

   f. General-purpose cable routing assemblies

(3) Types FPLP, FPLR, and FPL cables installed in a raceway of a type recognized in Chapter 3

760.136 Separation from Power Conductors

(A) General. Power-limited fire alarm conductors must not be placed in any enclosure, raceway, or cable with conductors of electric light, power, or Class 1 circuits.

(B) Separated by Barriers. If separated by a barrier, power-limited fire alarm circuits are permitted with electric power conductors.

Author's Comment:

■ Separation is required to prevent a fire or shock hazard that can occur from a short between the fire alarm circuit and the higher-voltage circuits.

(D) Associated Systems Within Enclosures. Power-limited fire alarm conductors can be mixed with electric light, power, and Class 1 circuit conductors in enclosures where these other conductors are introduced solely for connection to the same equipment, and:

(1) A minimum of ¼ in. separation is maintained from the power-limited fire alarm cable conductors.

(G) Other Applications. Power-limited fire alarm circuit conductors must be separated by not less than 2 in. from insulated conductors of electric light, power, or Class 1 circuits unless:

(1) Electric light, power, Class 1 circuit conductors, or power-limited fire alarm circuit conductors, are in a raceway or in metal-sheathed, metal-clad, nonmetallic-sheathed, or underground feeder cables. Figure 760–19

760.139 Power-Limited Fire Alarm Circuits, Class 2, Class 3, and Communications Circuits

(A) Two or More PLFA Circuits. Power-limited fire alarm circuits, communications circuits, or Class 3 circuits can be in the same cable, enclosure, cable tray, raceway, or cable routing assembly. Figure 760–20

(B) PLFA and Class 2 Circuits. Class 2 circuits can be within the same cable, cable routing assembly, enclosure, cable tray, or raceway as conductors of power-limited fire alarm circuits provided the Class 2 circuit conductor insulation isn't less than that required for the power-limited fire alarm circuits.

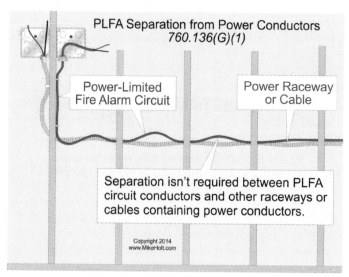

Figure 760-19

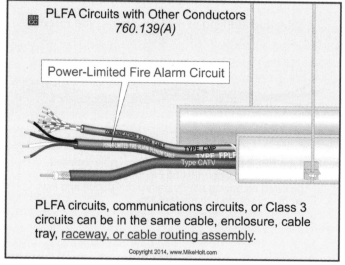

Figure 760-20

Author's Comment:

- Listed Class 2 cables have an insulation voltage rating of at least 150V [725.179(G)], whereas listed power-limited fire alarm cables have a voltage rating of not less than 300V [760.179(C)].

(D) Audio System Circuits and Power-Limited Fire Alarm Circuits. Audio system circuits [640.9(C)] using Class 2 or Class 3 wiring methods [725.133 and 725.154] must not be installed in the same cable, cable routing assembly, cable tray, or raceway with power-limited fire alarm conductors or cables.

Author's Comment:

- The concern is that a fault from audio amplifier circuits to fire alarm circuits has the potential to create a hazard by disrupting the operation of fire alarm systems. However, this restriction doesn't apply to the voice annunciation audio circuits supplied and controlled from a fire alarm panel and commonly required in high-rise buildings and similar applications.

760.143 Support

Power-limited fire alarm cables aren't permitted to be strapped, taped, or attached to the exterior of any raceway as a means of support. Figure 760-21

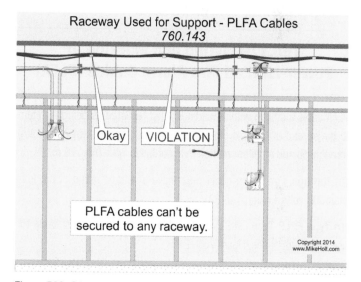

Figure 760-21

760.154 Applications of Power-Limited Fire Alarm Cables (PLFA)

PLFA cables must meet the requirements of Table 760.154, or the substitutions allowed in 760.154(A). Figure 760-22

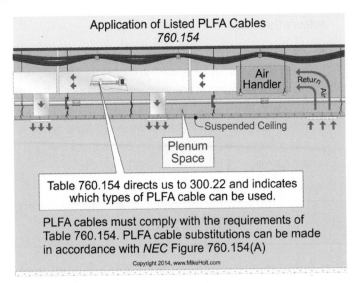

Figure 760–22

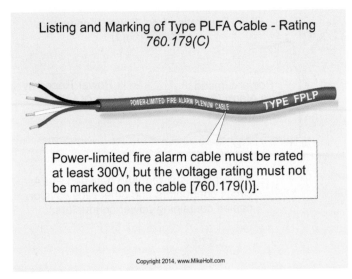

Figure 760–23

Part IV. Listing Requirements

760.179 Listing and Marking of Power-Limited Fire Alarm Cables (PLFA)

PLFA cable installed within buildings must be listed as being resistant to the spread of fire and other criteria in accordance with 760.179(A) through (H) and shall be marked in accordance with 760.179 (I).

(C) Ratings. Fire Alarm cable must have a voltage rating of not less than 300 volts. Figure 760–23

(D) Type FPLP. Type FPLP plenum cable is listed as being suitable for use in plenum space. Figure 760–24

(I) Marking. Cables must be marked in accordance with Table 760.179(I). Voltage ratings are not permitted to be marked on the cable.

> **Note:** Voltage markings on cables may suggest that the cables are suitable for Class 1 or electric power and light applications, which they are not.

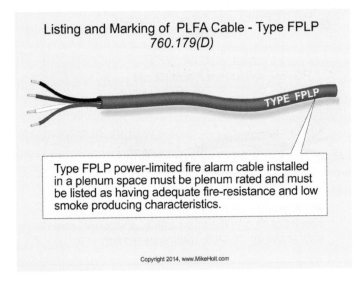

Figure 760–24

ARTICLE 760 PRACTICE QUESTIONS

Please use the 2014 *Code* book to answer the following questions.

1. Article 760 covers the requirements for the installation of wiring and equipment of _____.

   (a) communications systems
   (b) antennas
   (c) fire alarm systems
   (d) fiber optics

2. Fire alarm systems include _____.

   (a) fire detection and alarm notification
   (b) guard's tour
   (c) sprinkler waterflow
   (d) all of these

3. Fire alarm cables that are not terminated at equipment and not identified for future use with a tag are considered abandoned.

   (a) True
   (b) False

4. If fire alarm conductors are installed in a raceway that is subjected to different temperatures, and where condensation is known to be a problem, the raceway must be filled with a material approved by the authority having jurisdiction that will prevent the circulation of warm air to a colder section of the raceway. An explosionproof seal _____.

   (a) is required for this purpose
   (b) has been proven effective for this purpose
   (c) isn't required for this purpose
   (d) is the only method of doing this

5. Raceways enclosing cables and conductors for fire alarm systems must be large enough to permit the _____ of conductors without damaging conductor insulation as limited by 300.17.

   (a) installation
   (b) removal
   (c) splicing
   (d) a and b

6. When a raceway is used for the support or protection of cables for fire alarm circuits, a bushing to reduce the potential for abrasion must be placed at the location the cables enter the raceway.

   (a) True
   (b) False

7. Exposed fire alarm circuit cables shall be supported by the building structure using straps, staples, hangers, cable ties or similar fittings designed and installed so as not to damage the cable.

   (a) True
   (b) False

8. Accessible portions of abandoned fire alarm cable shall be removed.

   (a) True
   (b) False

9. Fire alarm cables identified for future use shall be marked with a tag of sufficient durability to withstand _____.

   (a) moisture
   (b) humidity
   (c) the environment involved
   (d) none of these

10. Fire alarm circuits shall be identified at all terminal and junction locations in a manner that helps prevent unintentional signals on fire alarm system circuits during _____ of other systems.

    (a) installation
    (b) testing and servicing
    (c) renovations
    (d) all of these

11. The fire alarm circuit disconnecting means for a power-limited fire alarm system must _____.

    (a) have red identification
    (b) be accessible only to qualified personnel
    (c) be identified as "FIRE ALARM CIRCUIT"
    (d) all of these

12. The power source for a power-limited fire alarm circuit can be supplied through a ground-fault circuit interrupter or an arc-fault circuit interrupter.

    (a) True
    (b) False

13. Fire alarm equipment supplying power-limited fire alarm circuits shall be durably marked where plainly visible to indicate each circuit that is _____.

    (a) supplied by a nonpower-limited fire alarm circuit
    (b) a power-limited fire alarm circuit
    (c) a fire alarm circuit
    (d) none of these

14. Cable splices or terminations in power-limited fire alarm systems shall be made in listed _____ or utilization equipment.

    (a) fittings
    (b) boxes or enclosures
    (c) fire alarm devices
    (d) any of these

15. Generally speaking, conductors for lighting or power may occupy the same enclosure or raceway with conductors of power-limited fire alarm circuits.

    (a) True
    (b) False

16. Cables and conductors of two or more power-limited fire alarm circuits can be installed in the same cable, enclosure, cable tray, raceway, or cable routing assembly.

    (a) True
    (b) False

17. Audio system circuits using Class 2 or Class 3 wiring methods shall not be installed in the same cable, raceway, or cable routing assembly with _____.

    (a) other audio system circuits
    (b) power-limited fire alarm conductors or cables
    (c) a or b
    (d) none of these

18. Power-limited fire alarm cables can be supported by strapping, taping, or attaching to the exterior of a conduit or raceway.

    (a) True
    (b) False

19. Power-limited fire alarm cables installed within buildings shall be _____ as being resistant to the spread of fire.

    (a) marked FR
    (b) listed
    (c) identified
    (d) color-coded

20. Power-limited fire alarm cable used in a _____ location shall be listed for use in _____ locations or have a moisture-impervious metal sheath.

    (a) dry
    (b) damp
    (c) wet
    (d) hazardous

ARTICLE 770

OPTICAL FIBER CABLES AND RACEWAYS

Introduction to Article 770—Optical Fiber Cables and Raceways

Article 770 provides the requirements for installing optical fiber cables and special raceways for optical fiber cables. It also contains the requirements for composite cables, often called "hybrid," that combine optical fibers with current-carrying conductors.

While we normally think of Article 300 in connection with wiring methods, you only need to use the Article 770 methods for optical fiber cables, except where it makes specific references to Article 300 [770.3]. For instance, in 770.113, reference is made to 300.22, which applies when installing optical fiber cables and optical fiber raceways in ducts and plenum spaces.

This article doesn't refer to 300.15, so boxes aren't required for splices or terminations of optical fiber cable. Note 1 to 770.48 states that splice cases and terminal boxes are typically used as enclosures for splicing or terminating optical fiber cables.

Article 90 states that the *NEC* isn't a design guide or installation manual. Thus, Article 770 doesn't deal with the performance of optical fiber systems. For example, it doesn't mention cable bending radii. It doesn't explain how to install and test cable safely either, but that doesn't mean you should look into an optical fiber cable, even if you can't see any light coming through it. Light used in these circuits usually isn't visible, but it can still damage your eyes.

Part I. General

770.1 Scope

Article 770 covers the installation of optical fiber cables, which transmit light for control, signaling, and communications. This article also contains the installation requirements for optical fiber raceways and cable routing assemblies, as well as the requirements for composite cables that combine optical fibers with current-carrying conductors. Figure 770–1

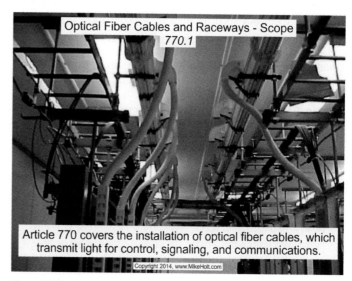

Optical Fiber Cables and Raceways - Scope
770.1

Article 770 covers the installation of optical fiber cables, which transmit light for control, signaling, and communications.

Copyright 2014, www.MikeHolt.com

Figure 770–1

Author's Comment:

- The growth of high-tech applications and significant technological development of optical fibers and the equipment used to send and receive light pulses has increased the use of optical fibers. Since optical fiber cable isn't affected by electromagnetic interference, there's been a large growth in its uses in communications for voice, data transfer, data processing, and computer control of machines and processes.

770.2 Definitions

Abandoned Optical Fiber Cable. A cable that isn't terminated to equipment and not identified for future use with a tag.

Author's Comment:

- Section 770.25 requires the accessible portion of abandoned cables to be removed.

Composite Optical Fiber Cable. A cable containing optical fibers and current-carrying electrical conductors.

Author's Comment:

- Article 770 permits the use of composite cables only where the optical fibers and current-carrying electrical conductors are functionally associated [770.133(A)].

Conductive Optical Fiber Cable. An optical fiber cable containing conductive members such as metallic strength members, metallic vapor barriers, or metallic armor or sheath. Figure 770–2

Innerduct. A nonmetallic raceway placed within a larger raceway. Figure 770–3

Nonconductive Optical Fiber Cable. A factory assembly of one or more optical fibers containing no electrically conductive materials. Figure 770–4

Optical Fiber Cable. A factory assembly or field assembly of optical fibers having an overall covering. Figure 770–5

Note: A field-assembled optical fiber cable is an assembly of one or more optical fibers within a jacket. The jacket is installed like a raceway, and then the optical fibers are inserted into it.

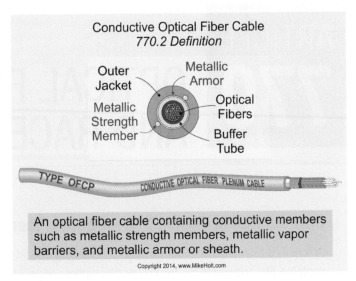

Figure 770–2

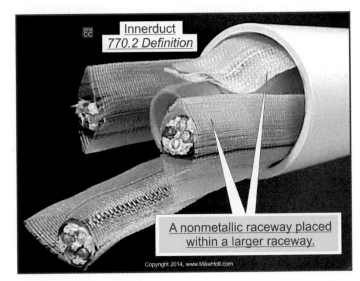

Figure 770–3

Point of Entrance. The point within a building at which the optical fiber cable emerges from an external wall, from a concrete floor slab, or from rigid metal conduit or intermediate metal conduit.

770.3 Other Articles

Only those sections in Chapter 2 and Article 300 referenced in Article 770 apply to optical fiber cables and raceways.

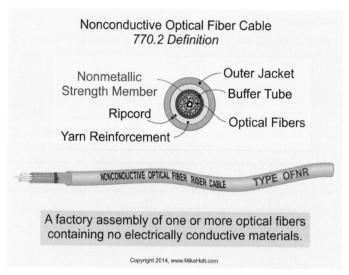

Figure 770–4

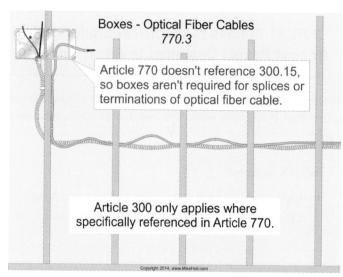

Figure 770–6

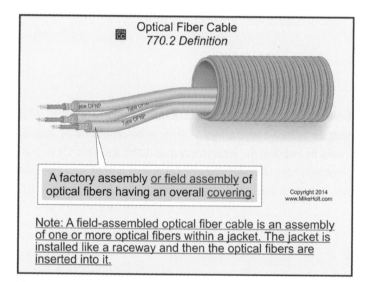

Figure 770–5

Author's Comment:

■ Article 770 doesn't reference 300.15, so boxes aren't required for splices or terminations of optical fiber cable. Figure 770–6

On the other hand, composite (hybrid) optical fiber cables [770.2] are considered electrical cables and must comply with the appropriate requirements of the *NEC* Chapters 1 through 4.

770.12 Innerduct

Listed communications raceways selected in accordance with the provisions of Table 800.154(b) can be installed as innerduct in any Chapter 3 raceway. Figure 770–7

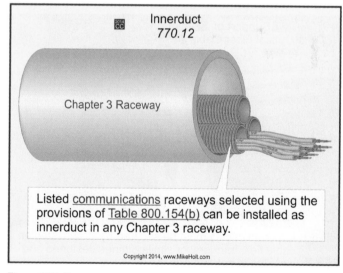

Figure 770–7

770.21 Access to Electrical Equipment Behind Panels Designed to Allow Access

Access to equipment must not be prohibited by an accumulation of optical fiber cables that prevent the removal of suspended-ceiling panels.

Author's Comment:

■ Cables must be located so that the suspended-ceiling panels can be moved to provide access to electrical equipment.

770.24 Mechanical Execution of Work

Equipment and cabling must be installed in a neat and workmanlike manner. Exposed cables must be supported by the structural components of the building so that the cable won't be damaged by normal building use. Such cables must be secured by straps, staples, hangers, cable ties, or similar fittings designed and installed in a manner that won't damage the cable, and be installed in accordance with 300.4(D) through (G) and 300.11. Figure 770–8

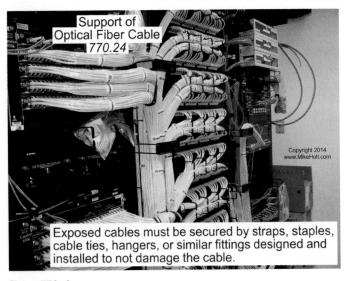

Figure 770–8

Communications raceways and cable assemblies must be securely fastened in place and the ceiling-support wires or ceiling grid must not be used to support optical fiber raceways or cables [300.11]. Figure 770–9

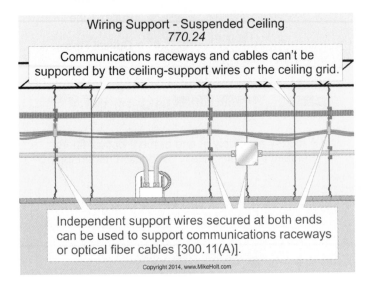

Figure 770–9

Cables installed through or parallel to framing members or furring strips must be protected where they're likely to be penetrated by nails or screws by installing the wiring method so it isn't less than 1¼ in. from the nearest edge of the framing member or furring strips, or is protected by a ¹⁄₁₆ in. thick steel plate or the equivalent [300.4(D)]. Figure 770–10

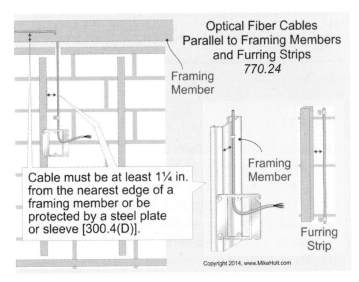

Figure 770–10

Cable ties used to secure or support optical fiber cables in plenums must be listed for use in plenums. Figure 770–11

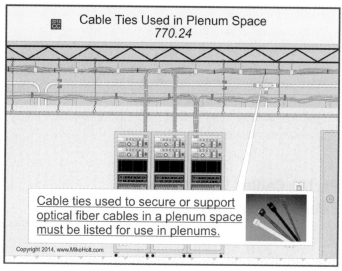

Figure 770–11

Note 1: Accepted industry practices are described in ANSI/NECA/BICSI 568, *Standard for Installing Commercial Building Telecommunications Cabling* and ANSI/NECA/FOA 301, *Standard for Installing and Testing Fiber Optic Cables.* Figure 770–12

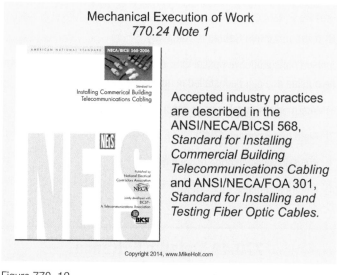

Figure 770–12

Author's Comment:

- For more information about these standards, visit www. NECA-NEIS.org.

Note 2: See 4.3.11.2.6.5 and 4.3.11.5.5.6 of NFPA 90A, *Standard for the Installation of Air-Conditioning and Ventilating Systems*, for discrete combustible components installed in accordance with 300.22(C).

770.25 Abandoned Cable

To limit the spread of fire or products of combustion within a building, the accessible portion of cable that isn't terminated at equipment and not identified for future use with a tag must be removed [770.2]. Figure 770–13

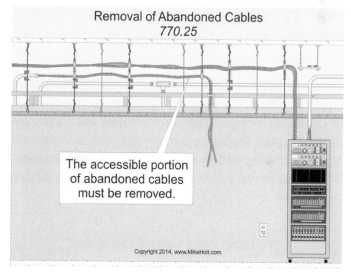

Figure 770–13

Cables identified for future use must be with a tag that can withstand the environment involved. Figure 770–14

Author's Comment:

- Cables installed in concealed raceways aren't considered "accessible"; therefore, they're not required to be removed.

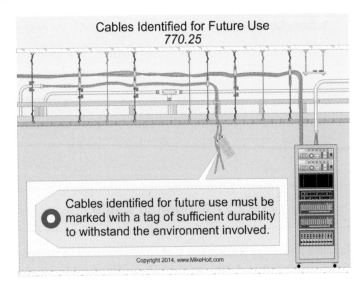

Figure 770-14

770.26 Spread of Fire or Products of Combustion

Optical fiber cables and communications raceways must be installed in such a way that the spread of fire or products of combustion won't be substantially increased. Openings in fire-rated walls, floors, and ceilings for optical fiber cables and communications raceways must be firestopped using methods approved by the authority having jurisdiction to maintain the fire-resistance rating of the fire-rated assembly. Figure 770-15

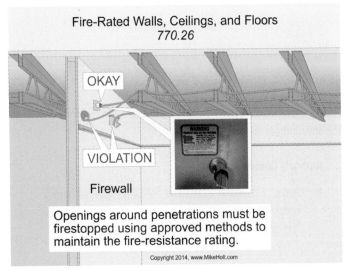

Figure 770-15

Author's Comment:

■ Firestop material is listed for the specific types of wiring methods and construction structures.

Note: Directories of electrical construction materials published by qualified testing laboratories contain many listing installation restrictions necessary to maintain the fire-resistive rating of assemblies. Outlet boxes must have a horizontal separation not less than 24 in. when installed in a fire-rated assembly, unless an outlet box is listed for closer spacing or protected by fire-resistant "putty pads" in accordance with manufacturer's instructions.

Part II. Cables Outside and Entering Buildings

770.48 Unlisted Cables and Raceways Entering Buildings

(A) Conductive and Nonconductive Cables. Unlisted optical fiber cables can be installed in building spaces, other than risers, ducts, or plenum spaces, if the length of the optical fiber cable measured from its point of entrance doesn't exceed 50 ft and the optical fiber cable terminates in an enclosure.

Note 2: See 770.2 for the definition of *Point of Entrance.*

(B) Nonconductive Cables in Raceway.

Unlisted nonconductive optical fiber cables can enter the building from the outside and can be installed in any of the following raceways:

(1) Intermediate metal conduit (IMC)

(2) Rigid metal conduit (RMC)

(3) Rigid polyvinyl chloride conduit (PVC)

(4) Electrical metallic tubing (EMT)

770.49 Metallic Entrance Conduit Grounding

Rigid metal conduit (RMC) or intermediate metal conduit (IMC) containing optical fiber entrance cable must be connected to a grounding electrode in accordance with 770.100(B).

Part V. Installation Methods Within Buildings

770.110 Raceways and Cable Routing Assemblies for Optical Fiber Cables

(A) Types of Raceways.

(1) Chapter 3 Raceways. Optical fiber cables can be installed in any Chapter 3 raceway in accordance with the requirements of Chapter 3.

(2) Communications Raceways. Optical fiber cables can be installed in a listed communications raceway selected in accordance with the provisions of 770.113, 800.110, and 800.113, and installed in accordance with 362.24 through 362.56. Figure 770–16

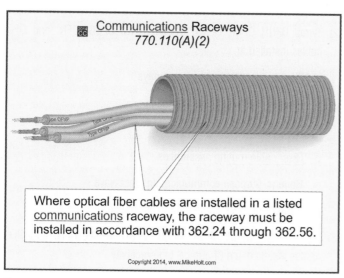

Communications Raceways
770.110(A)(2)

Where optical fiber cables are installed in a listed communications raceway, the raceway must be installed in accordance with 362.24 through 362.56.

Copyright 2014, www.MikeHolt.com

Figure 770–16

Author's Comment:

- In other words, listed communications raceways must be installed according to the following ENT rules:

  - 362.24 Bending radius
  - 362.26 Maximum total bends between pull points, 360 degrees
  - 362.28 Trimmed to remove rough edges
  - 362.30 Support every 3 ft, within 3 ft of any enclosure
  - 362.48 Joints between tubing, fittings, and boxes

- A communications raceway is an enclosed channel of non-metallic materials designed for holding communications wire and cables, optical fiber cables, and Class 2 and 3 circuits [Article 100]. Figure 770–17

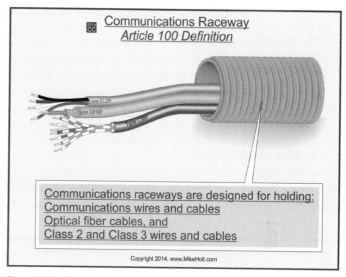

Communications Raceway
Article 100 Definition

Communications raceways are designed for holding:
Communications wires and cables
Optical fiber cables, and
Class 2 and Class 3 wires and cables

Copyright 2014, www.MikeHolt.com

Figure 770–17

(B) Raceway Fill for Optical Fiber Cables.

(1) Without Electric Light or Power Conductors. If optical fiber cables are installed in a raceway without current-carrying conductors, the raceway fill tables of Chapters 3 and 9 don't apply.

(C) Cable Routing Assemblies. Optical fiber cables can be installed in cable routing assemblies in accordance with 800.113 and Table 800.154(c). They must also be supported in accordance with the following:

(1) Horizontal Support. Where installed horizontally, cable routing assemblies must be supported every 3 ft, and at each end or joint, unless listed otherwise. The distance between supports can never exceed 10 ft.

(2) Vertical Support. Where installed vertically, cable routing assemblies must be supported every 4 ft, unless listed otherwise, and must not have more than one joint between supports.

770.113 Installation of Optical Fiber Cables

(A) Listing. Optical fiber cables installed within buildings must be listed.

Ex: Unless the length of the cable from its point of entrance, doesn't exceed 50 ft as permitted by 770.48.

Author's Comment:

- The *NEC* doesn't require outside or underground cable to be listed, but the cable must be approved by the authority having jurisdiction as suitable for the application in accordance with 90.4, 90.7, and 110.2.

(C) Plenum Spaces. The following cables are permitted in plenum spaces described in 300.22(C): Figure 770–18

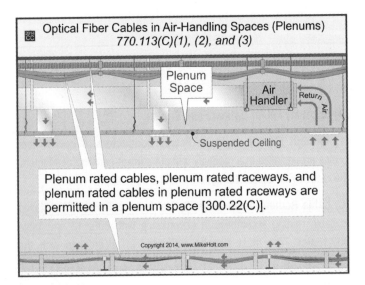

Figure 770–18

(1) Types OFNP and OFCP cables

(2) Types OFNP and OFCP cables installed in plenum communications raceways

(3) Types OFNP and OFCP cables supported by open metallic cable trays or cable tray systems

(4) Types OFNP, OFCP, OFNR, OFCR, OFNG, OFCG, OFN, and OFC cables installed in raceways that are installed in accordance with 300.22(C).

(H) Cable Trays. The following cables can be installed in cable trays:

(1) Types OFNP, OFCP, OFNR, OFCR, OFNG, OFCG, OFN, and OFC cables

(2) Types OFNP, OFCP, OFNR, OFCR, OFNG, OFCG, OFN, and OFC cables installed in:

    a. Plenum communications raceways

    b. Riser communications raceways

    c. General-purpose communications raceways

(J) Other Building Locations. The following cables are permitted in the spaces not described in 770.113(B) through (I):

(1) Types OFNP, OFCP, OFNR, OFCR, OFNG, OFCG, OFN, and OFC cables

(2) Types OFNP, OFCP, OFNR, OFCR, OFNG, OFCG, OFN, and OFC cables installed in:

    a. Plenum communications raceways

    b. Plenum cable routing assemblies

    c. Riser communications raceways

    d. Riser cable routing assemblies

    e. General-purpose communications raceways

    f. General-purpose cable routing assemblies

(3) Types OFNP, OFCP, OFNR, OFCR, OFNG, OFCG, OFN, and OFC cables installed in a Chapter 3 type raceway

770.133 Installation of Optical Fiber Cables and Electrical Conductors

(A) With Power Conductors. Optical fibers are permitted within the same composite cable with power circuits, if the functions of the optical fibers and the electrical conductors are associated.

Nonconductive optical fiber cables are permitted to occupy the same cable tray or raceway with conductors for electric light, power, and Class 1 circuits. Figure 770–19

Nonconductive optical fiber cables can't occupy a cabinet, outlet box, panel, or similar enclosure housing the electrical terminations of an electric light, power, or Class 1 circuit.

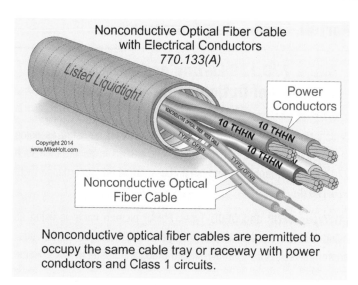

Nonconductive optical fiber cables are permitted to occupy the same cable tray or raceway with power conductors and Class 1 circuits.

Figure 770–19

Ex 1: Nonconductive optical fiber cables are permitted to occupy the same cabinet, outlet box, panel, or similar enclosure housing the electrical terminations of an electric light, power, or Class 1 circuit, if the nonconductive optical fiber cable is functionally associated with the electric light, power, or Class 1 circuit.

(B) With Communications Cables. Optical fiber cables can be in the same raceway, cable tray, box, enclosure, or cable routing assembly, with conductors of any of the following: Figure 770–20

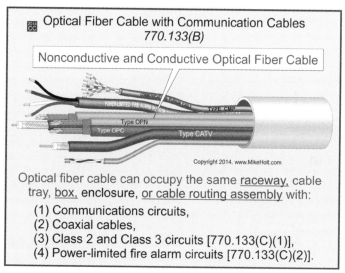

Optical fiber cable can occupy the same raceway, cable tray, box, enclosure, or cable routing assembly with:
(1) Communications circuits,
(2) Coaxial cables,
(3) Class 2 and Class 3 circuits [770.133(C)(1)],
(4) Power-limited fire alarm circuits [770.133(C)(2)].

Figure 770–20

(1) Communications circuits in accordance with Parts I and V of Article 800.

(2) Coaxial cables in accordance with Parts I and V of Article 820.

(C) With Other Circuits. Optical fiber cables can be in the same raceway, cable tray, box, cable routing assembly, or enclosure with conductors of any of the following:

(1) Class 2 and Class 3 remote-control, signaling, and power-limited circuits in accordance with Parts I and III of Article 725 or in accordance with Article 645.

(2) Power-limited fire alarm circuits in accordance with Parts I and III of Article 760.

(D) Support of Cables. Optical fiber cables aren't permitted to be strapped, taped, or attached to the exterior of any raceway as a means of support. Figure 770–21

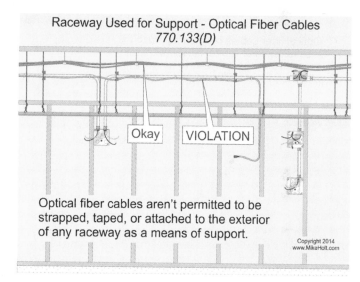

Optical fiber cables aren't permitted to be strapped, taped, or attached to the exterior of any raceway as a means of support.

Figure 770–21

770.154 Applications of Listed Optical Fiber Cables

Listed optical fiber cables must be installed as indicated in Table 770.154(a), as limited by 770.110 and 770.113, and cable substitutions in accordance with Table 770.154(b). Figure 770–22

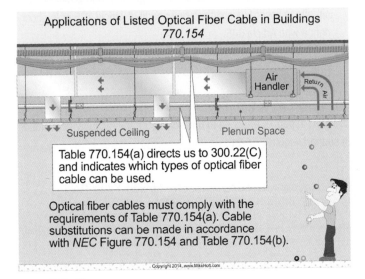

Figure 770–22

Part VI. Listing Requirements

770.179 Listing and Marking of Optical Fiber Cables

Optical fiber cable installed within buildings must be listed as being resistant to the spread of fire and other criteria in accordance with 770.179(A) through (H) and shall be marked in accordance with 770.179 (I).

(A) Types OFNP and OFCP. Types PLFAP plenum cable is listed as being suitable for use in plenum space and listed as having adequate fire-resistance and low-smoke producing characteristics. Figure 770–23

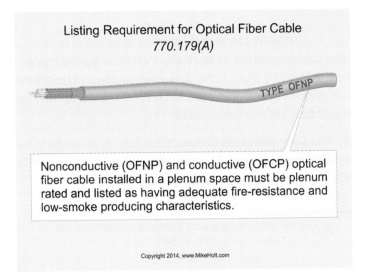

Figure 770–23

ARTICLE 770 PRACTICE QUESTIONS

Please use the 2014 *Code* book to answer the following questions.

1. Optical fiber cables not terminated at equipment, and not identified for future use with a tag are considered abandoned.

   (a) True
   (b) False

2. Composite optical fiber cables contain optical fibers and _____.

   (a) strength members
   (b) vapor barriers
   (c) current-carrying electrical conductors
   (d) none of these

3. Conductive optical fiber cables contain noncurrent-carrying conductive members such as metallic _____.

   (a) strength members
   (b) vapor barriers
   (c) armor or sheath
   (d) any of these

4. Nonconductive optical fiber cable is a factory assembly of one or more optical fibers with an overall covering and containing no electrically conductive materials.

   (a) True
   (b) False

5. Nonconductive optical fiber cable contains no metallic members and no other _____ materials.

   (a) electrically conductive
   (b) inductive
   (c) synthetic
   (d) insulating

6. The point of entrance of an optical fiber installation is the point _____ at which the optical fiber cable emerges from an external wall, from a concrete floor slab, from rigid metal conduit, or from intermediate metal conduit.

   (a) outside a building
   (b) within a building
   (c) on the building
   (d) none of these

7. Access to electrical equipment shall not be denied by an accumulation of optical fiber cables that _____ removal of panels, including suspended-ceiling panels.

   (a) prevents
   (b) hinders
   (c) blocks
   (d) require

8. Optical fiber cables installed _____ on the surface of ceilings and walls shall be supported by the building structure in such a manner that the cable will not be damaged by normal building use.

   (a) exposed
   (b) concealed
   (c) hidden
   (d) a and b

9. Exposed optical fiber cables shall be supported by the building structure using hardware including straps, staples, cable ties, hangers, or similar fittings designed and installed so as not to damage the cable.

    (a) True
    (b) False

10. Accepted industry practices for optical fiber installations are described in _____.

    (a) ANSI/NECA/BICSI 568, *Standard for Installing Commercial Building Telecommunications Cabling*
    (b) ANSI/NECA/FOA 301, *Standard for Installing and Testing Fiber Optic Cables*
    (c) other ANSI-approved installation standards
    (d) all of these

11. Accessible portions of abandoned optical fiber cable shall be removed.

    (a) True
    (b) False

12. Openings around penetrations of optical fiber cables and communications raceways through fire-resistant–rated walls, partitions, floors, or ceilings shall be _____ using approved methods to maintain the fire-resistance rating.

    (a) closed
    (b) opened
    (c) draft stopped
    (d) firestopped

13. Optical fiber cables are not required to be listed and marked where the length of the cable within the building, measured from its point of entrance, does not exceed _____ ft and the cable enters the building from the outside and is terminated in an enclosure.

    (a) 25
    (b) 30
    (c) 50
    (d) 100

14. Unlisted conductive and nonconductive outside plant optical fiber cables shall be permitted to be installed in locations other than risers, ducts used for environmental air, plenums used for environmental air, and other spaces used for environmental air, where the length of the cable within the building, measured from its point of entrance, does not exceed _____ ft and the cable enters the building from the outside and is terminated in an enclosure.

    (a) 25
    (b) 50
    (c) 75
    (d) 100

15. When optical fiber cable is installed in a Chapter 3 raceway, the raceway shall be installed in accordance with Chapter 3 requirements.

    (a) True
    (b) False

16. Optical fibers shall be permitted within the same composite cable as electric light, power, and Class 1 circuits operating at 1,00V, or less where the functions of the optical fibers and the electrical conductors are associated.

    (a) True
    (b) False

17. Conductive optical fiber cables can occupy the same cable tray, raceway, box, enclosure, or cable routing assembly with conductors for electric light, power, and Class 1 circuits.

    (a) True
    (b) False

18. Optical fiber cables shall not be _____ to the exterior of any conduit or raceway as a means of support.

    (a) strapped
    (b) taped
    (c) attached
    (d) all of these

ARTICLE 800

COMMUNICATIONS CIRCUITS

Introduction to Article 800—Communications Circuits

This article has its roots in telephone technology. Consequently, it addresses telephone and related systems that use twisted-pair wiring. Here are a few key points to remember about Article 800:

- Don't attach incoming communications cables to the service-entrance power mast.
- It's critical to determine the "point of entrance" for these circuits.
- Ground the primary protector as close as practicable to the point of entrance.
- Keep the grounding electrode conductor for the primary protector as straight and as short as possible.
- If you locate communications cables above a suspended ceiling, route and support them to allow access via ceiling panel removal.
- Keep these cables separated from lightning protection circuits.
- If you install communications cables in a Chapter 3 raceway, you must do so in conformance with the *NEC* requirements for the raceway system.
- Special labeling and marking provisions apply—follow them carefully.

Part I. General

800.1 Scope

This article covers communications circuits that extend voice, audio, video, interactive services, and outside wiring for fire alarms and burglar alarms from the communications utility to the customer's communications equipment up to and including equipment such as a telephone, fax machine, or answering machine [800.2], and communications equipment. Figure 800–1

Author's Comment:

- The definition of "communications equipment" is contained in Article 100.

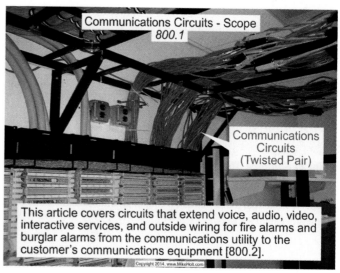

Communications Circuits - Scope
800.1

Communications Circuits (Twisted Pair)

This article covers circuits that extend voice, audio, video, interactive services, and outside wiring for fire alarms and burglar alarms from the communications utility to the customer's communications equipment [800.2].

Figure 800–1

800.2 Definitions

Abandoned Communications Cable. A communications cable that isn't terminated to equipment and not identified for future use with a tag.

Author's Comment:

- Section 800.25 requires the accessible portion of abandoned communications cables to be removed.

Communications Circuit. The circuit that extends voice, audio, video, data, interactive services, and outside wiring for fire alarms and burglar alarms from the communications utility to the customer's communications equipment up to and including terminal equipment such as a telephone, fax machine, or answering machine.

Innerduct. A nonmetallic raceway placed within a larger raceway. Figure 800–2

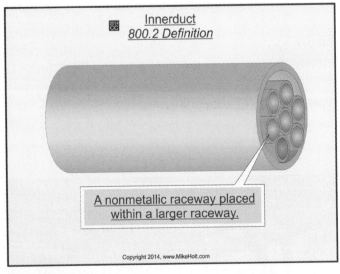

Figure 800–2

Point of Entrance. The point within a building at which the communications cable emerges from an external wall, from a concrete floor slab, or from a rigid metal conduit (RMC) or an intermediate metal conduit (IMC). Figure 800–3

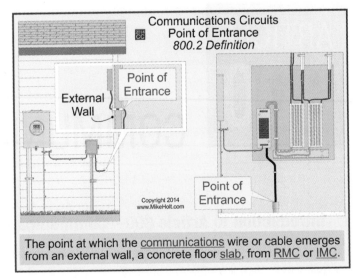

The point at which the communications wire or cable emerges from an external wall, a concrete floor slab, from RMC or IMC.

Figure 800–3

800.12 Innerduct

Listed communications raceways selected in accordance with Table 800.154(b) can be installed as innerduct in any Chapter 3 raceway. Figure 800–4

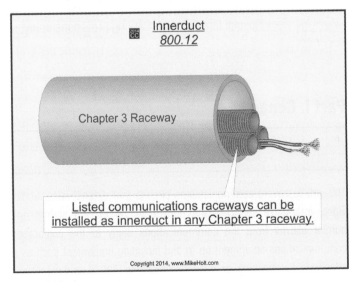

Figure 800–4

800.18 Installation of Equipment

Communications equipment must be listed in accordance with 800.170.

800.21 Access to Electrical Equipment Behind Panels Designed to Allow Access

Access to equipment must not be prohibited by an accumulation of communications cables that prevent the removal of suspended-ceiling panels.

800.24 Mechanical Execution of Work

Equipment and communications cabling must be installed in a neat and workmanlike manner. Exposed communications cables must be supported by the structural components of the building so that the communications cable won't be damaged by normal building use. Cables must be secured with straps, staples, cable ties, hangers, or similar fittings designed and installed so as not to damage the communications cable. Figure 800–5

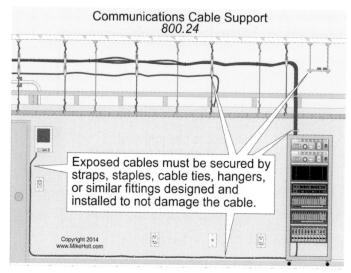

Figure 800–5

Communications raceways and communications cable assemblies must be securely fastened in place and ceiling-support wires or the ceiling grid must not be used to support communications raceways or communications cables [300.11]. Figure 800–6

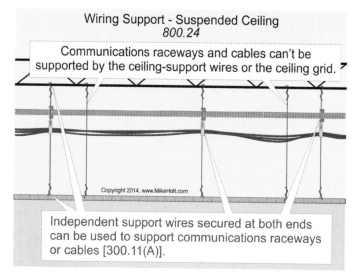

Figure 800–6

Author's Comment:

■ Raceways and cables can be supported by independent support wires attached to the suspended ceiling in accordance with 300.11(A).

Cables installed parallel to framing members or furring strips must be protected where they're likely to be penetrated by nails or screws, by installing the wiring method so it isn't less than 1¼ in. from the nearest edge of the framing member or furring strips, or is protected by a ¹⁄₁₆ in. thick steel plate or the equivalent [300.4(D)]. Figure 800–7

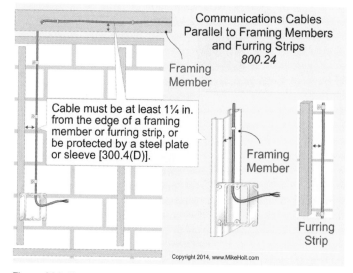

Figure 800–7

Cable ties used to secure or support communications cables in plenums must be listed for use in plenums. Figure 800–8

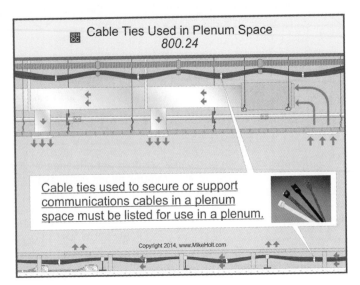

Figure 800–8

Note 1: Accepted industry practices are described in ANSI/NECA/BICSI 568, *Standard for Installing Commercial Building Telecommunications Cabling*, ANSI/TIA 569, *Commercial Building Standard for Telecommunications Pathways and Spaces*, ANSI/TIA 570-B, *Residential Telecommunications Infrastructure*, and other ANSI standards. Figure 800–9

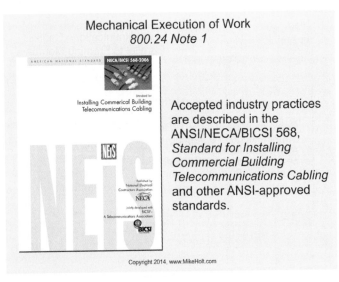

Figure 800–9

Author's Comment:

- For more information about these standards, visit www. NECA-NEIS.org.

Note 2: See 4.3.11.2.6.5 and 4.3.11.5.5.6 of NFPA 90A-2009, *Standard for the Installation of Air-Conditioning and Ventilating Systems*, for discrete combustible components installed in accordance with 300.22(C).

800.25 Abandoned Cable

To limit the spread of fire or products of combustion within a building, the accessible portion of communications cable that isn't terminated at equipment and not identified for future use with a tag must be removed [800.2]. Figure 800–10

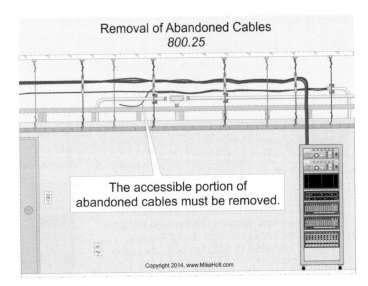

Figure 800–10

Author's Comment:

- Cables installed in concealed raceways aren't considered "accessible"; therefore, they're not required to be removed.

Cables identified for future use must be with a tag that can withstand the environment involved. Figure 800–11

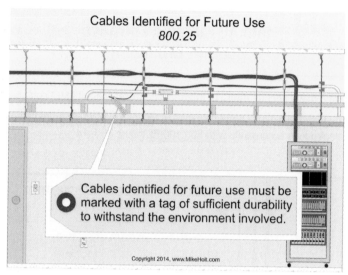

Figure 800–11

800.26 Spread of Fire or Products of Combustion

Communications circuits and equipment must be installed in such a way that the spread of fire or products of combustion won't be substantially increased. Openings in fire-rated walls, floors, and ceilings for communications cables, communications raceways, and cable routing assemblies must be firestopped using methods approved by the authority having jurisdiction to maintain the fire-resistance rating of the fire-rated assembly. Figure 800–12

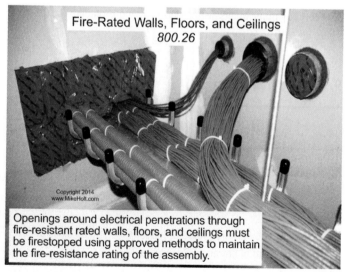

Figure 800–12

Author's Comment:

- Firestop material is listed for the specific types of wiring methods and construction structures.

Note: Directories of electrical construction materials published by qualified testing laboratories contain listing and installation restrictions necessary to maintain the fire-resistive rating of assemblies. For example, outlet boxes must have a horizontal separation not less than 24 in. when installed in a fire-rated assembly, unless an outlet box is listed for closer spacing or protected by fire-resistant "putty pads" in accordance with manufacturer's instructions.

Part II. Cables Outside and Entering Buildings

800.44 Overhead (Aerial) Communications Wires and Cables

(B) Above Roofs. Overhead (aerial) communications cables must have a vertical clearance of at least 8 ft from all points of roofs above which they pass.

Ex 1: Auxiliary buildings such as garages.

Ex 2: Cable clearance over the roof overhang can be reduced from 8 ft to 18 in. if no more than 6 ft of overhead (aerial) conductors pass over no more than 4 ft of roof and they terminate to a raceway mast or other approved support.

800.47 Underground Communications Wires and Cables Entering Buildings

The requirements that insulated conductors and cables in wet locations be listed for wet locations [310.10(C)] don't apply to communications cables.

800.48 Unlisted Cables Entering Buildings

Unlisted communications cables can be installed in building spaces other than risers, ducts, or plenum spaces as described in 300.22(C), if the length of the cable within the building from its point of entrance doesn't exceed 50 ft and the cable terminates in an enclosure or primary protector. Figure 800–13

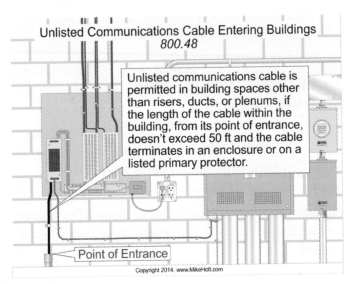

Figure 800–13

Note 2: The primary protector must be located as close as practicable to the point at which the cable enters the building [800.90(B)]. Therefore, unlisted outside plant communications cables may not be permitted to enter the building if it's practicable to place the primary protector closer than 50 ft to the point of entrance.

Author's Comment:

- The "point of entrance" is defined as the point within the building where the cable emerges from an external wall, from a concrete floor slab, or from rigid metal conduit or intermediate metal conduit connected to an electrode by a grounding conductor in accordance with 800.100 [800.2].

800.49 Metallic Entrance Conduit Grounding

Rigid metal conduit (RMC) or intermediate metal conduit (IMC) containing communications entrance cable must be connected to a grounding electrode in accordance with 800.100(B). Figure 800–14

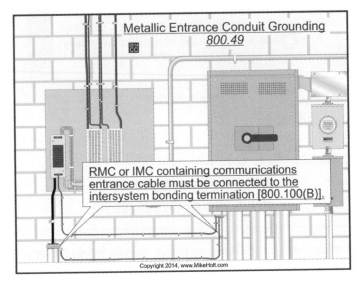

Figure 800–14

800.53 Lightning Conductors

If feasible, a separation of not less than 6 ft must be maintained between communications wiring and lightning protection conductors. Figure 800–15

Part III. Protection

800.90 Primary Protection

(A) Application. A listed primary protector is required for each communications circuit, and it must be installed in accordance with 110.3(B). Figure 800–16

(B) Location. The primary protector must be located as close as practicable to the point of entrance. See Figure 800–16.

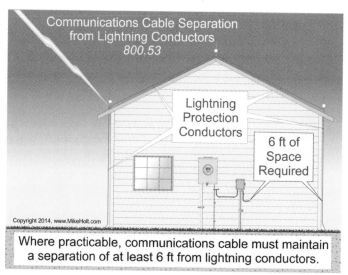

Where practicable, communications cable must maintain a separation of at least 6 ft from lightning conductors.

Figure 800–15

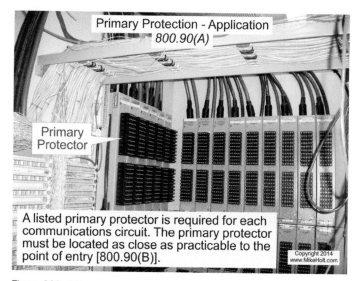

A listed primary protector is required for each communications circuit. The primary protector must be located as close as practicable to the point of entry [800.90(B)].

Figure 800–16

Note: The point of entrance is defined as the point within the building where the communications cable emerges from an external wall, from a concrete floor slab, or from a rigid metal conduit or an intermediate metal conduit connected to an electrode by a grounding electrode conductor in accordance with 800.100 [800.2].

Author's Comment:

■ Selecting a primary protector location to achieve the shortest practicable primary protector bonding conductor or grounding electrode conductor helps reduce differences in potential between communications circuits and other metallic systems during lightning events.

Part IV. Grounding Methods

800.100 Cable and Primary Protector Bonding and Grounding

The primary protector and the metallic member of cable sheaths must be bonded or grounded in accordance with (A) through (D).

(A) Bonding Conductor or Grounding Electrode Conductor.

(1) Insulation. The conductor must be listed and can be insulated, covered, or bare.

(2) Material. The conductor must be copper or other corrosion-resistant conductive material, stranded or solid.

(3) Size. The conductor must not be smaller than 14 AWG with a current-carrying capacity of not less than the grounded metallic sheath member(s) or protected conductor(s) of the communications cable, but not required to be larger than 6 AWG.

(4) Length. The bonding conductor or grounding electrode conductor must be as short as practicable. For one- and two-family dwellings, the bonding conductor or grounding electrode conductor must not exceed 20 ft in length. Figure 800–17

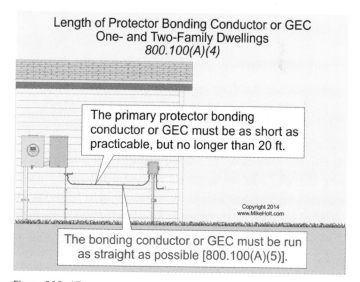

Figure 800–17

Note: Limiting the length of the bonding conductor or grounding electrode conductor helps limit induced potential (voltage) differences between the building's power and communications systems during lightning events.

Ex: If the bonding conductor or grounding electrode conductor is over 20 ft in length for one- and two-family dwellings, a separate rod not less than 5 ft long [800.100(B)(3)(2)] with fittings suitable for the application [800.100(C)] must be installed. The additional rod must be bonded to the power grounding electrode system with a minimum 6 AWG conductor [800.100(D)]. Figure 800–18

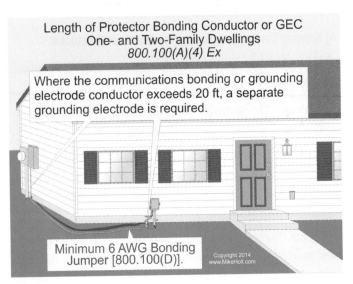

Length of Protector Bonding Conductor or GEC One- and Two-Family Dwellings 800.100(A)(4) Ex

Where the communications bonding or grounding electrode conductor exceeds 20 ft, a separate grounding electrode is required.

Minimum 6 AWG Bonding Jumper [800.100(D)].

Copyright 2014 www.MikeHolt.com

Figure 800–18

(5) Run in Straight Line. Run in as straight a line as practicable.

Author's Comment:

- Lightning doesn't like to travel around corners or through loops, which is why the grounding electrode conductor or bonding jumper must be run as straight as practicable.

(6) Physical Protection. The bonding conductor and grounding electrode conductor must not be subject to physical damage. If installed in a metal raceway, both ends of the raceway must be bonded to the contained conductor or connected to the same terminal or electrode to which the bonding conductor or grounding electrode conductor is connected.

Author's Comment:

- Installing the bonding conductor or grounding electrode conductor in PVC conduit is a better practice.

(B) Electrode. The bonding conductor or grounding electrode conductor must be connected in accordance with (B)(1), (B)(2), or (B)(3):

(1) Buildings with an Intersystem Bonding Termination. The bonding conductor for the primary protector and the metallic sheath of communications cable must terminate to the intersystem bonding termination as required by 250.94. Figure 800–19

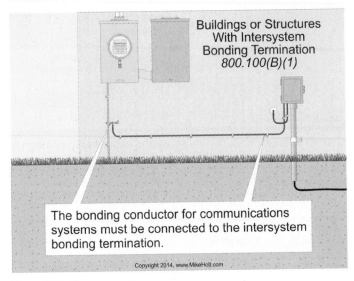

Buildings or Structures With Intersystem Bonding Termination 800.100(B)(1)

The bonding conductor for communications systems must be connected to the intersystem bonding termination.

Copyright 2014, www.MikeHolt.com

Figure 800–19

Author's Comment:

- According to the Article 100 definition, an "Intersystem Bonding Termination" is a device that provides a means to connect intersystem bonding conductors for communications systems to the grounding electrode system. Figure 800–20

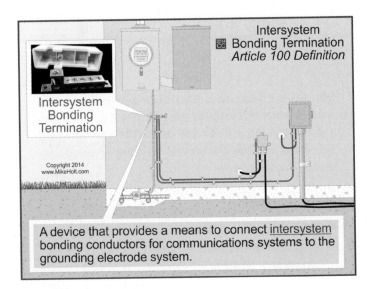

Intersystem Bonding Termination Article 100 Definition

Intersystem Bonding Termination

Copyright 2014 www.MikeHolt.com

A device that provides a means to connect intersystem bonding conductors for communications systems to the grounding electrode system.

Figure 800–20

(2) Building Without Intersystem Bonding Termination. The bonding conductor or grounding electrode conductor must terminate to the nearest accessible: Figure 800–21

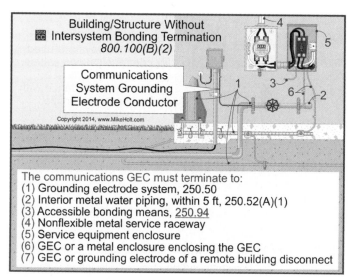

Figure 800–21

(1) Building grounding electrode system [250.50].

(2) Interior metal water piping system, within 5 ft from its point of entrance [250.52(A)(1)].

(3) Accessible means external to the building, as covered in 250.94.

(4) Nonflexible metallic service raceway.

(5) Service equipment enclosure.

(6) Grounding electrode conductor or the grounding electrode conductor metal enclosure of the power service.

(7) Grounding electrode conductor or the grounding electrode of a remote building disconnecting means [250.32].

The intersystem bonding termination must be mounted on the fixed part of an enclosure so that it won't interfere with the opening of an enclosure door. A bonding device must not be mounted on a door or cover even if the door or cover is nonremovable.

(3) In Buildings Without Intersystem Bonding Termination or Grounding Means. The grounding electrode conductor must connect to:

(1) Any individual grounding electrodes described in 250.52(A)(1), (A)(2), (A)(3), or (A)(4).

(2) Any individual grounding electrode described in 250.52(A)(7) and (A)(8), or to a rod not less than 5 ft long and ½ in. diameter located not less than 6 ft from electrodes of other systems. Figure 800–22

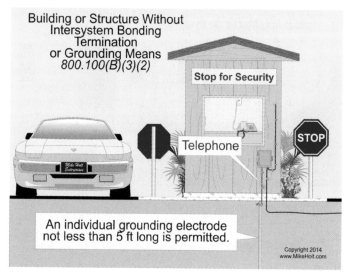

Figure 800–22

Author's Comment:

■ The reason communications rods only need to be 5 ft long is because that's the length the telephone company used before the *NEC* contained requirements for communications systems. Telephone company rods were only 5 ft long because that's the length that would fit in their equipment trailers.

(C) Electrode Connection. Terminations at the grounding electrode must be by exothermic welding, listed lugs, listed pressure connectors, or listed clamps. Grounding fittings that are concrete-encased or buried in the earth must be listed for direct burial [250.70].

(D) Bonding of Electrodes. If a separate grounding electrode, such as a rod, is installed for a communications system, it must be bonded to the building's power grounding electrode system with a minimum 6 AWG conductor. Figure 800–23

Note 2: Bonding of electrodes helps reduce induced potential (voltage) between the power and communications systems during lightning events. Figure 800–24

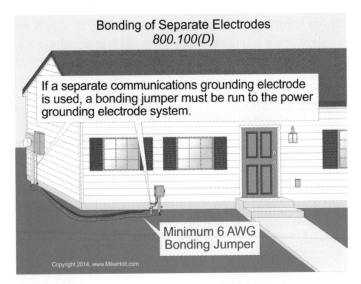

Figure 800–23

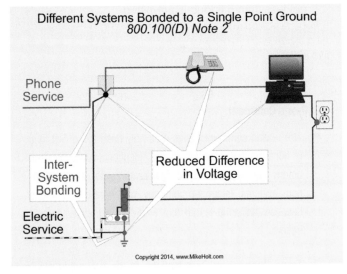

Figure 800–24

Part V. Installation Methods Within Buildings

800.110 Raceways and Cable Routing Assemblies for Communications Wires and Cables

(A) Types of Raceways.

(1) Chapter 3 Raceways. Communications cables can be installed in any Chapter 3 raceway in accordance with the requirements of Chapter 3. Figure 800–25

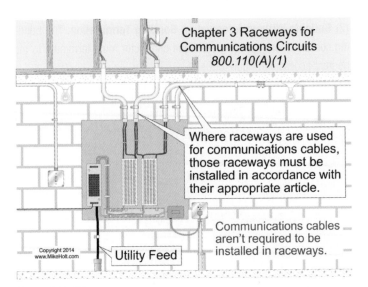

Figure 800–25

(2) Communications Raceways. Communications cables can be installed in a listed communications raceway selected in accordance with 800.113. If communications cables are installed in a listed communications nonmetallic raceway, the raceway must be installed in accordance with 362.24 through 362.56. Figure 800–26

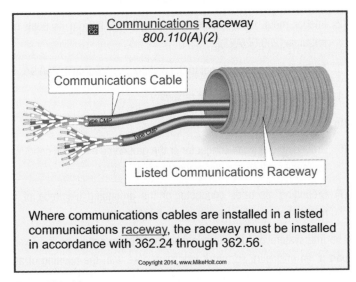

Figure 800–26

Author's Comment:

- In other words, listed communications raceways must be installed in accordance with the following rules for ENT:

    □ 362.24 Bending radius

    □ 362.26 Maximum total bends between pull points, 360 degrees

    □ 362.28 Trimmed to remove rough edges

    □ 362.30 Supported every 3 ft, and within 3 ft of any enclosure

    □ 362.48 Joints between tubing, fittings, and boxes

Author's Comment:

- A communications raceway is an enclosed channel of non-metallic materials designed for holding communications wire and cables, optical fiber cables and Class 2 and 3 circuits [Article 100]. Figure 800–27

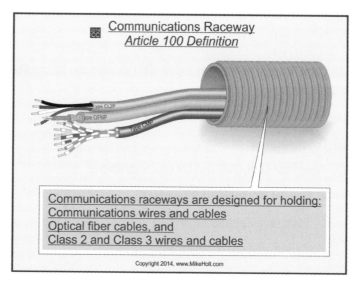

Figure 800–27

(B) Raceway Fill for Communications Wires and Cables. Raceway fill limitations of 300.17 don't apply to communications cables installed in a raceway.

(C) Cable Routing Assemblies. Communications cables can be installed in cable routing assemblies in accordance with 800.113 and must installed in accordance with the following:

(1) Horizontal Support. Where installed horizontally, cable routing assemblies must be supported every 3 ft, and at each end or joint, unless listed otherwise. The distance between supports can never exceed 10 ft.

(2) Vertical Support. Where installed vertically, cable routing assemblies must be supported every 4 ft, unless listed otherwise, and must not have more than one joint between supports.

800.113 Installation of Communications Cables, Raceways, and Cable Routing Assemblies

(A) Listing. Communications cables, raceways, and cable routing assemblies installed within buildings must be listed.

Ex: Unless the length of the cable from its point of entrance doesn't exceed 50 ft as permitted by 800.48.

(C) Plenum Spaces.

(1) Plenum Rated Cables. Exposed plenum rated communications cables (CMP) are permitted in plenum spaces as described in 300.22(C): Figure 800–28

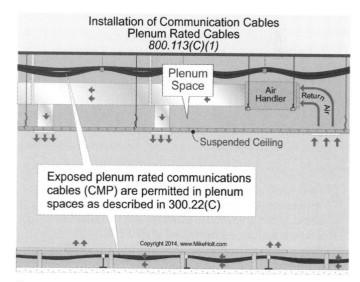

Figure 800–28

(2) Plenum Rated Raceways. Exposed plenum rated communications raceways are permitted in plenum spaces as described in 300.22(C): Figure 800–29

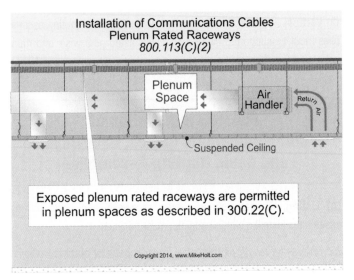

Figure 800–29

(3) Plenum Rated Cables in Plenum Rated Raceways. Plenum rated communications cables in plenum rated raceways are permitted in plenum spaces as described in 300.22(C): Figure 800–30

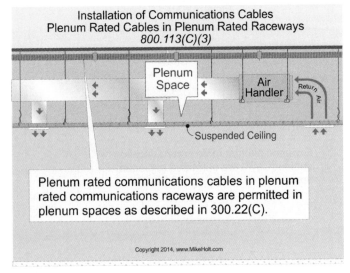

Figure 800–30

(5) Non-Plenum Rated Cables. Non-plenum rated communications cables and wires installed in metal raceways are permitted in plenum spaces as described in 300.22(C). Figure 800–31

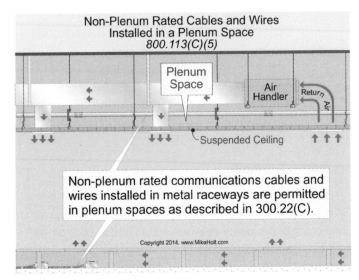

Figure 800–31

(H) Cable Trays. The following cables and raceways can be installed in cable trays:

(1) Types CMP, CMR, CMG, and CM cables

(2) Communications raceways

(3) Types CMP, CMR, CMG, and CM cables installed in:

    a. Plenum communications raceways

    b. Riser communications raceways

    c. General-purpose communications raceways

(J) Other Building Locations. The following cables and raceways can be installed in building locations other than those covered in 800.113(B) through (I):

(1) Types CMP, CMR, CMG, and CM cables

(2) A maximum of 10 ft of exposed Type CMX cable in nonconcealed spaces

(3) Communications raceways

(4) Cable routing assemblies

(6) Types CMP, CMR, CMG, and CM cables installed in:

    a. Plenum cable routing assemblies

    b. Riser cable routing assemblies

    c. General-purpose cable routing assemblies

(7) Listed communications wires and Types CMP, CMR, CMG, CM, and CMX cables and installed in a Chapter 3 raceway

(L) One- and Two-Family Dwellings. The following cables, raceways, and cable routing assemblies can be installed in one- and two-family dwellings in locations other than the locations covered in 800.113(B) through (F):

(1) Types CMP, CMR, CMG, and CM cables

(2) Type CMX cables less than ¼ in. in diameter

(3) Plenum, riser, and general-purpose communications raceways

(4) Cable routing assemblies

(6) Types CMP, CMR, CMG, and CM cables installed in:

    a. Plenum cable routing assemblies

    b. Riser cable routing assemblies

    c. General-purpose cable routing assemblies

(7) Listed communication wires and Types CMP, CMR, CMG, CM, and CMX cables installed in raceways recognized in Chapter 3

800.133 Installation of Communications Wires, Cables, and Equipment

(A) Separation from Power Conductors.

(1) In Raceways, Cable Routing Assemblies, Cable Trays, and Enclosures. Figure 800–32

(a) With Optical Fiber Cables. Communications cables can be in the same raceway, cable tray, box, cable routing assembly, or enclosure with cables of any of the following:

(1) Optical fiber cables in accordance with Parts I and V of Article 770.

(2) Coaxial cables in accordance with Parts I and V of Article 820.

(b) With Other Circuits. Communications cables can be in the same raceway, cable tray, cable routing assembly, box, or enclosure with cables of any of the following:

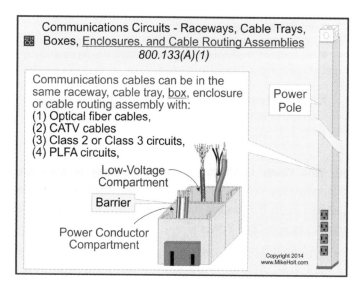

Figure 800–32

(1) Class 2 and Class 3 circuits in accordance with Article 645 or Parts I and III of Article 725.

(2) Power-limited fire alarm circuits in accordance with Parts I and III of Article 760.

(c) Class 2 and Class 3 Circuits. Class 2 or Class 3 conductors can be within the same cable with communications conductors, provided that the cables is communications rated in accordance with Article 800 [725.139(D)(1)]. Figure 800–33

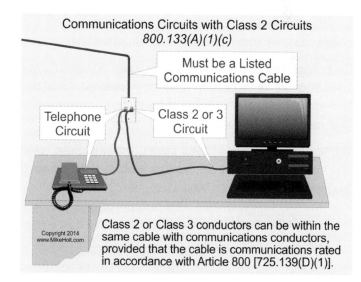

Figure 800–33

Author's Comment:

■ A common application of this requirement is when a single cable is used for both voice communications and data.

■ Listed Class 2 cables have a voltage rating of not less than 150V [725.179(G)], whereas communications cables have a voltage rating of at least 300V [800.179].

(d) With Power Conductors in Same Raceway or Enclosure. Communications conductors must not be placed in any raceway, compartment, outlet box, junction box, or similar fitting with conductors of electric power or Class 1 circuits.

Ex 1: Communications circuits can be within the same enclosure with conductors of electric power and Class 1 circuits where separated by a permanent barrier or listed divider.

Author's Comment:

■ Separation is required to prevent a fire or shock hazard that can occur from a short between the communications circuits and the higher-voltage circuits.

Ex 2: Communications conductors can be mixed with power conductors if the power circuit conductors are only introduced to supply power to communications equipment. The power circuit conductors must maintain a minimum ½ in. separation from the communications circuit conductors.

(2) Other Applications. Communications circuits must maintain 2 in. of separation from electric power or Class 1 circuit conductors.

Ex 1: Separation isn't required if electric power or Class 1 circuit conductors are in a raceway or in metal-sheathed, metal-clad, nonmetallic-sheathed, or underground feeder cables, or communications cables are in a raceway. Figure 800–34

(B) Support of Communications Cables. Communications cables aren't permitted to be strapped, taped, or attached to the exterior of any raceway as a means of support. Figure 800–35

Author's Comment:

■ Exposed cables must be supported by the structural components of the building so that the cable won't be damaged by normal building use. The cables must be secured by straps, staples, cable ties, hangers, or similar fittings designed and installed in a manner that won't damage the cable [800.24].

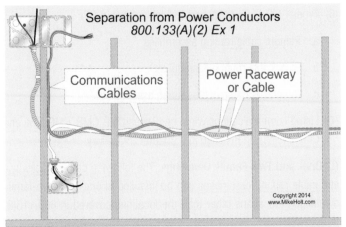

Separation from Power Conductors
800.133(A)(2) Ex 1

Communications Cables

Power Raceway or Cable

Copyright 2014
www.MikeHolt.com

Cable separation isn't required from power conductors that are installed in a Chapter 3 wiring method.

Figure 800–34

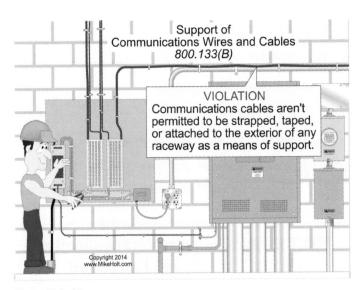

Support of Communications Wires and Cables
800.133(B)

VIOLATION
Communications cables aren't permitted to be strapped, taped, or attached to the exterior of any raceway as a means of support.

Copyright 2014
www.MikeHolt.com

Figure 800–35

Ex: Aerial spans of communications cable can be attached to the exterior of a raceway mast. Figure 800–36

800.154 Applications of Communications Cables, Communications Raceways, and Cable Routing Assemblies

Listed communications cables, raceways, and cable routing assemblies can be installed in accordance with:

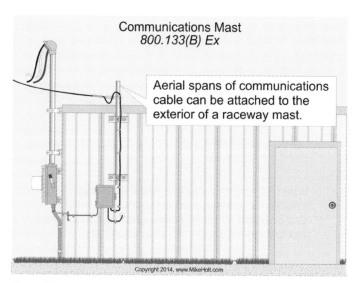

Figure 800–36

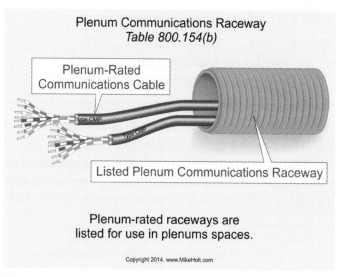

Figure 800–38

(1) Listed plenum rated communications wires and cables are permitted in plenum spaces as indicated in Table 800.154(a). Figure 800–37

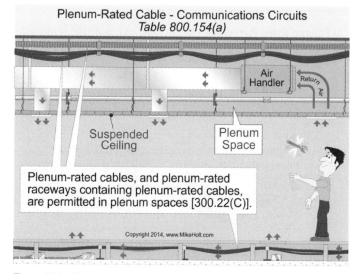

Figure 800–37

(2) Listed plenum rated communications raceways are permitted in plenum spaces as indicated in Table 800.154(b). Figure 800–38

(3) Listed cable routing assemblies as indicated in Table 800.154(c).

Cable substitutions may be made in accordance with Table 800.154(d).

800.156 Dwelling Unit Communications Outlet

One communications outlet must be installed in a readily accessible area within each dwelling unit and cabled to the service provider's demarcation point. Figure 800–39

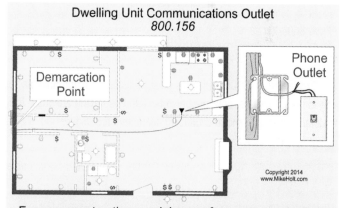

Figure 800–39

Part VI. Listing Requirements

800.179 Listing and Marking of Communications Wires and Cables

Communications wires and cables must be listed in accordance with 800.179(A) through (I) and marked in accordance with Table 800.179. Communications wires and cables must have a voltage rating of not less than 300 volts. The cable voltage rating must not be marked on the cable or on the undercarpet communications wire. Figure 800–40

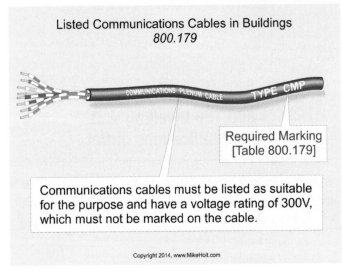

Listed Communications Cables in Buildings
800.179

Required Marking
[Table 800.179]

Communications cables must be listed as suitable for the purpose and have a voltage rating of 300V, which must not be marked on the cable.

Copyright 2014, www.MikeHolt.com

Figure 800–40

(A) Type CMP. Type CMP plenum cable is listed as being suitable for use in plenum space, and must also be listed as having adequate fire-resistance and low smoke-producing characteristics. Figure 800–41

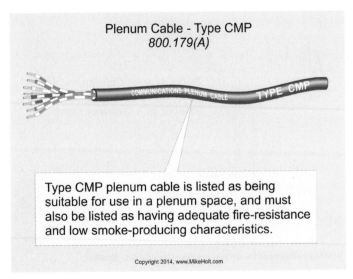

Plenum Cable - Type CMP
800.179(A)

Type CMP plenum cable is listed as being suitable for use in a plenum space, and must also be listed as having adequate fire-resistance and low smoke-producing characteristics.

Copyright 2014, www.MikeHolt.com

Figure 800–41

800.182 Listing and Marking of Communications Raceways

(A) Plenum Rated Raceways. Plenum rated communications raceways are listed as being suitable for use in plenum space. Figure 800–42

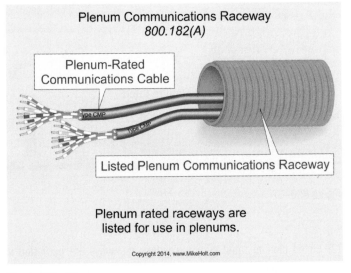

Plenum Communications Raceway
800.182(A)

Plenum-Rated
Communications Cable

Listed Plenum Communications Raceway

Plenum rated raceways are listed for use in plenums.

Copyright 2014, www.MikeHolt.com

Figure 800–42

ARTICLE 800 PRACTICE QUESTIONS

Please use the 2014 *Code* book to answer the following questions.

1. Communications cables not terminated at both ends with a connector or other equipment and not identified for future use with a tag are considered abandoned.

   (a) True
   (b) False

2. The circuit that extends voice, audio, video, interactive services, telegraph (except radio), and outside wiring for fire alarm and burglar alarm from the communications utility to the customer's communications equipment up to and including equipment such as a telephone, fax machine or answering machine defines a "_____ circuit."

   (a) limited-energy
   (b) remote-signaling
   (c) power-limited
   (d) communications

3. Communications circuits are circuits that extend _____ and outside wiring for fire alarms and burglar alarms from the communications utility to the customer's communications equipment up to and including equipment such as a telephone, fax machine, or answering machine.

   (a) voice
   (b) audio and video
   (c) interactive services
   (d) all of these

4. Equipment intended to be permanently electrically connected to a communications network shall be listed.

   (a) True
   (b) False

5. Access to electrical equipment shall not be denied by an accumulation of communications _____ that prevents the removal of suspended-ceiling panels.

   (a) wires
   (b) cables
   (c) ductwork
   (d) a and b

6. Communications cables installed _____ on the surface of ceilings and walls shall be supported by the building structure in such a manner that the cable will not be damaged by normal building use.

   (a) exposed
   (b) concealed
   (c) hidden
   (d) a and b

7. Exposed communications cables shall be secured by hardware including straps, staples, cable ties, hangers, or similar fittings designed and installed so as not to damage the cable.

   (a) True
   (b) False

8. Accessible portions of abandoned communications cable shall be removed.

    (a) True
    (b) False

9. Openings around penetrations of communications cables, communications raceways, and cable routing assemblies through fire-resistant–rated walls, partitions, floors, or ceilings shall be _____ using approved methods to maintain the fire-resistance rating.

    (a) closed
    (b) opened
    (c) draft stopped
    (d) firestopped

10. Outside plant communications cables shall not be required to be listed where the length of the cable within the building, measured from its point of entrance, does not exceed _____ ft and the cable enters the building from the outside and is terminated in an enclosure or on a listed primary protector.

    (a) 25
    (b) 30
    (c) 50
    (d) 100

11. When practicable, a separation of at least _____ ft shall be maintained between communications cables on buildings and lightning conductors.

    (a) 6
    (b) 8
    (c) 10
    (d) 12

12. In installations where the communications cable enters a building, the metallic sheath members of the cable shall be _____ as close as practicable to the point of entrance.

    (a) grounded as specified in 800.100
    (b) interrupted by an insulating joint or equivalent device
    (c) a or b
    (d) a and b

13. In one- and two-family dwellings, the primary protector bonding conductor or grounding electrode conductor for communications systems shall be as short as practicable, not to exceed _____ ft in length.

    (a) 5
    (b) 8
    (c) 10
    (d) 20

14. Limiting the length of the primary protector grounding conductors for communications circuits helps to reduce voltage between the building's _____ and communications systems during lightning events.

    (a) power
    (b) fire alarm
    (c) lighting
    (d) lightning protection

15. In one- and two-family dwellings where it is not practicable to achieve an overall maximum primary protector grounding electrode conductor length of 20 ft, a separate ground rod not less than _____ ft shall be driven and it shall be connected to the power grounding electrode system with a 6 AWG conductor.

    (a) 5
    (b) 8
    (c) 10
    (d) 20

16. For buildings with grounding means but without an intersystem bonding termination, the grounding conductor for communications circuits shall terminate to the nearest _____.

    (a) building or structure grounding electrode system
    (b) interior metal water piping system, within 5 ft from its point of entrance
    (c) service equipment enclosure
    (d) any of these

17. Communications grounding electrodes must be bonded to the power grounding electrode system at the building or structure served using a minimum _____ AWG copper bonding jumper.

    (a) 10
    (b) 8
    (c) 6
    (d) 4

18. Where communications wires and cables are installed in a Chapter 3 raceway, the raceway shall be installed in accordance with Chapter 3 requirements.

    (a) True
    (b) False

19. Communications wires, communications cables, communications raceways, and cable routing assemblies installed in buildings shall be listed except for up to 50 ft past the point of entry as allowed by 800.48.

    (a) True
    (b) False

20. Communications wires and cables shall be separated by at least 2 in. from conductors of _____ circuits, unless permitted otherwise.

    (a) power
    (b) lighting
    (c) Class 1
    (d) all of these

21. Type CMX communications cables can be installed in _____.

    (a) one- or two-family dwellings
    (b) multifamily dwellings in nonconcealed spaces
    (c) a or b
    (d) none of these

Mike Holt's Understanding 2014 NEC Requirements for Limited Energy & Communications Systems

RADIO AND TELEVISION EQUIPMENT

Introduction to Article 810—Radio and Television Equipment

This article covers transmitter and receiver equipment—and the wiring and cabling associated with that equipment. Here are a few key points to remember about Article 810:

- Avoid contact with conductors of other systems.
- Don't attach antennas or other equipment to the service-entrance power mast.
- Keep the bonding conductor or grounding electrode conductor as straight as practicable, and protect it from physical damage.
- If the mast isn't bonded properly, you risk flashovers and possible electrocution.
- Keep in mind that the purpose of bonding is to prevent a difference of potential between metallic objects and other conductive items, such as swimming pools.
- Clearances are critical, and Article 810 contains detailed clearance requirements. For example, it provides separate clearance requirements for indoor and outdoor locations.

Part I. General

810.1 Scope

Article 810 contains the installation requirements for the wiring of television and radio receiving equipment, such as digital satellite receiving equipment for television signals and amateur/citizen band radio equipment antennas. Figure 810–1

Author's Comment:

- Article 810 covers:
  - ☐ Antennas that receive local television signals.
  - ☐ Satellite antennas, which are often referred to as satellite dishes. Large satellite dish antennas (C Band dishes were 10 ft in diameter) usually have a motor that moves the dish to focus on different satellites. The smaller satellite dish antennas (18 in. in diameter) are usually aimed at a single satellite.

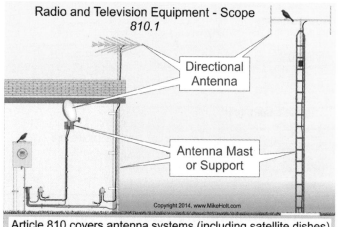

Radio and Television Equipment - Scope
810.1

Article 810 covers antenna systems (including satellite dishes) for radio and television receiving equipment, and amateur and citizen band radio transmitting and receiving equipment.

Figure 810–1

☐ Roof-mounted antennas for AM/FM/XM radio reception.

☐ Amateur radio transmitting and receiving equipment, including HAM radio equipment (a noncommercial [amateur] communications system).

810.3 Other Articles

Wiring from the power supply to Article 810 equipment must be installed in accordance with Chapters 1 through 4 except as modified by parts I and II of Article 640. Wiring for audio equipment must comply with Article 640, and coaxial cables that connect antennas to equipment must be installed in accordance with Article 820. Figure 810–2

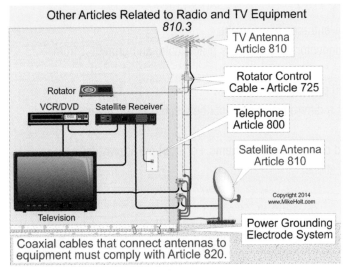

Figure 810–2

Author's Comment:

■ The grounding requirements for antenna cables are contained in 810.20(C) and 810.21, not Article 820.

810.4 Community Television Antenna

The antenna for community television systems must be installed in accordance with this article, but the coaxial cable beyond the point of entrance must be installed in accordance with Article 820. Figure 810–3

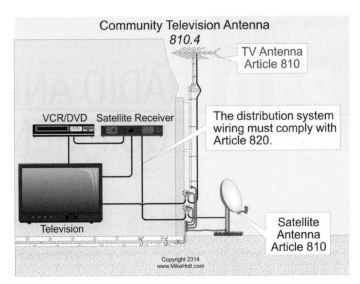

Figure 810–3

Author's Comment:

■ A community TV antenna is used for multiple-occupancy facilities, such as apartments, condominiums, motels, and hotels.

810.6 Antenna Lead-In Protectors

Antenna lead-in surge protectors must be listed, and must be grounded in accordance with 810.21. Figure 810–4

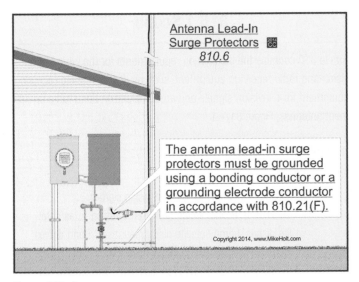

Figure 810–4

810.7 Grounding Devices

Fittings used to connect bonding jumpers or grounding electrode conductors to equipment must be listed.

Part II. Receiving Equipment— Antenna Systems

810.12 Supports

Outdoor antennas and lead-in conductors must be securely supported, and the lead-in conductors must be securely attached to the antenna. The antennas or lead-in conductors must not be attached to the electric service mast. Figure 810–5

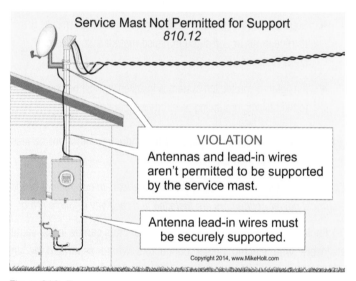

Service Mast Not Permitted for Support
810.12

VIOLATION
Antennas and lead-in wires aren't permitted to be supported by the service mast.

Antenna lead-in wires must be securely supported.

Copyright 2014, www.MikeHolt.com

Figure 810–5

810.13 Avoid Contact with Conductors of Other Systems

Outdoor antennas and lead-in conductors must be kept at least 2 ft from exposed electric power conductors to avoid the possibility of accidental contact.

Author's Comment:

■ According to the *National Electrical Code* Handbook, "One of the leading causes of electrical shock and electrocution is the accidental contact of radio, television, and amateur radio transmitting and receiving antennas, and equipment with light or power conductors. Extreme caution should therefore be exercised during this type of installation, and periodic visual inspections should be conducted thereafter."

810.15 Metal Antenna Supports—Grounding

Outdoor masts and metal structures that support antennas must be grounded in accordance with 810.21. Figure 810–6

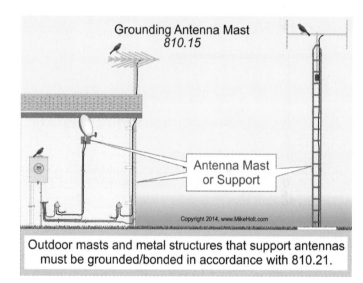

Grounding Antenna Mast
810.15

Antenna Mast or Support

Copyright 2014, www.MikeHolt.com

Outdoor masts and metal structures that support antennas must be grounded/bonded in accordance with 810.21.

Figure 810–6

810.18 Clearances

(A) Outside of Buildings. Lead-in conductors attached to buildings must be installed so that they can't swing closer than 2 ft to the conductors of circuits of 250V or less, or closer than 10 ft to the conductors of circuits of over 250V.

Lead-in conductors must be kept at least 6 ft from the lightning protection system and underground antenna lead-in conductors must maintain a separation not less than 12 in. from electric power conductors. Figure 810–7

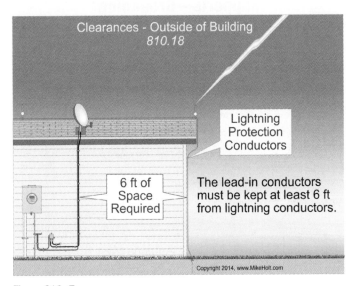

Figure 810–7

Ex: Separation isn't required where the underground antenna lead-in conductors or the electric power conductors are installed in raceways or cable armor. Figure 810–8

Author's Comment:

■ The *NEC* doesn't specify a burial depth for antenna lead-in wires.

Note 1: Air terminals for a lightning protection system must not be used for the building grounding electrode [250.60].

Note 2: Metal raceways, enclosures, frames, and metal parts of electric equipment must be bonded or spaced from the lightning protection system in accordance with NFPA 780, *Standard for the Installation of Lightning Protection Systems.*

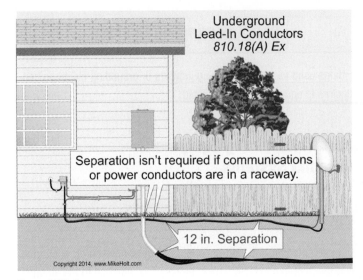

Figure 810–8

Author's Comment:

■ Separation from lightning protection conductors is typically 6 ft through air or 3 ft through dense materials such as concrete, brick, or wood.

■ If a lightning protection system is installed, it must be bonded to the building grounding electrode system [250.106].

(B) Indoors. Indoor antenna and lead-in conductors must not be less than 2 in. from electrical power conductors.

Ex 1: Separation isn't required if the antenna lead-in conductors or the electrical power conductors are installed in a raceway or cable armor.

(C) Enclosures. Indoor antenna lead-in conductors can be in the same enclosure with electric power conductors where separated by an effective, permanently installed barrier. Figure 810–9

810.20 Antenna Discharge Unit

(A) Where Required. Each lead-in conductor from an outdoor antenna must be provided with a listed antenna discharge unit. Figure 810–10

(B) Location. The antenna discharge unit must be located outside or inside the building, nearest the point of entrance, but not near combustible material or in a hazardous (classified) location as defined in Article 500.

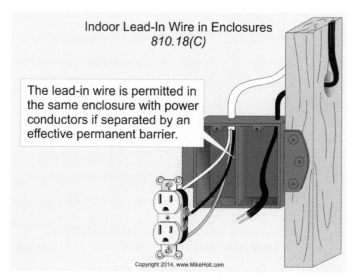

Indoor Lead-In Wire in Enclosures
810.18(C)

The lead-in wire is permitted in the same enclosure with power conductors if separated by an effective permanent barrier.

Copyright 2014, www.MikeHolt.com

Figure 810–9

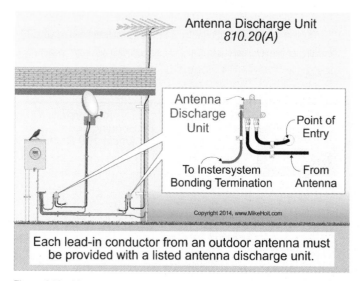

Antenna Discharge Unit
810.20(A)

Antenna Discharge Unit

Point of Entry

To Instersystem Bonding Termination

From Antenna

Copyright 2014, www.MikeHolt.com

Each lead-in conductor from an outdoor antenna must be provided with a listed antenna discharge unit.

Figure 810–10

(C) Grounding. The antenna discharge unit must be grounded in accordance with 810.21.

810.21 Bonding Conductor and Grounding Electrode Conductors

 Scan the QR code for a video clip of Mike explaining this topic; this is a sample from the DVDs that accompany this textbook.

The antenna mast [810.15] and antenna discharge unit [810.20(C)] must be grounded as follows.

Author's Comment:

- Grounding the lead-in antenna cables and the mast helps prevent voltage surges caused by static discharge or nearby lightning strikes from reaching the center conductor of the lead-in coaxial cable. Because the satellite dish sits outdoors, wind creates a static charge on the antenna as well as on the cable attached to it. This charge can build up on both the antenna and the cable until it jumps across an air space, often passing through the electronics inside the low noise block down converter feedhorn (LNBF) or receiver. Connecting the coaxial cable and dish to the building grounding electrode system (grounding) helps to dissipate this static charge.

  Nothing can prevent damage from a direct lightning strike, but grounding with proper surge protection can help reduce damage to the satellite dish and other equipment from nearby lightning strikes.

(A) Material. The bonding conductor or grounding electrode conductor to the electrode [810.21(F)] must be copper or other corrosion-resistant conductive material. Figure 810–11

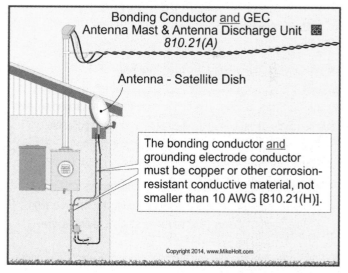

Bonding Conductor and GEC
Antenna Mast & Antenna Discharge Unit
810.21(A)

Antenna - Satellite Dish

The bonding conductor and grounding electrode conductor must be copper or other corrosion-resistant conductive material, not smaller than 10 AWG [810.21(H)].

Copyright 2014, www.MikeHolt.com

Figure 810–11

(B) Insulation. Insulated, covered, or bare.

(C) Supports. The bonding conductor or grounding electrode conductor must be securely fastened in place.

(D) Physical Protection. Bonding conductors or grounding electrode conductors must be mechanically protected where subject to physical damage, and where installed in a metal raceway, both ends of the raceway must be bonded to the bonding conductor or grounding electrode conductor. Figure 810–12

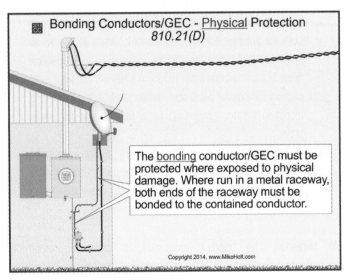

The bonding conductor/GEC must be protected where exposed to physical damage. Where run in a metal raceway, both ends of the raceway must be bonded to the contained conductor.

Figure 810–12

Author's Comment:

- Installing the bonding conductor or grounding electrode conductor in PVC conduit is a better practice.

(E) Run in Straight Line. The bonding conductor or grounding electrode conductor must be run in as straight a line as practicable.

Author's Comment:

- Lightning doesn't like to travel around corners or through loops, which is why the bonding conductor or grounding electrode conductor must be run as straight as practicable.

(F) Electrode. The bonding conductor or grounding electrode conductor must terminate in accordance with (1), (2), or (3).

(1) Buildings With an Intersystem Bonding Termination. The bonding conductor for the antenna mast and antenna discharge unit must terminate to the intersystem bonding termination as required by 250.94 [Article 100 and 250.94]. Figure 810–13

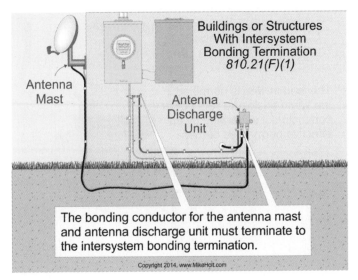

The bonding conductor for the antenna mast and antenna discharge unit must terminate to the intersystem bonding termination.

Figure 810–13

Note: According to the Article 100 definition, an Intersystem Bonding Termination is a device that provides a means to connect bonding conductors for communications systems to the grounding electrode system, in accordance with 250.94. Figure 810–14

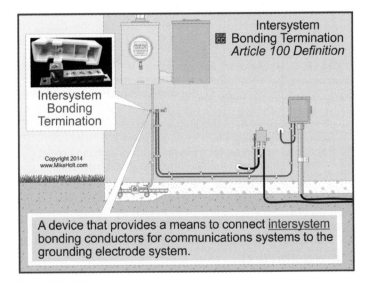

A device that provides a means to connect intersystem bonding conductors for communications systems to the grounding electrode system.

Figure 810–14

Author's Comment:

- Bonding all systems to the intersystem bonding termination helps reduce induced potential (voltage) differences between the power and the radio and television systems during lightning events. Figure 810–15

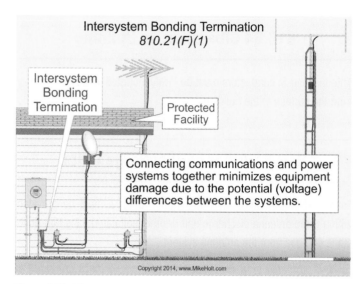

Figure 810–15

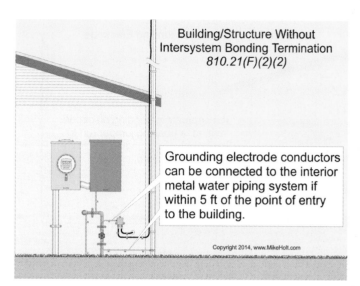

Figure 810–17

(2) In Buildings Without Intersystem Bonding Termination. The bonding conductor or grounding electrode conductor for the antenna mast and antenna discharge unit must terminate to the nearest accessible location on the following: Figure 810–16

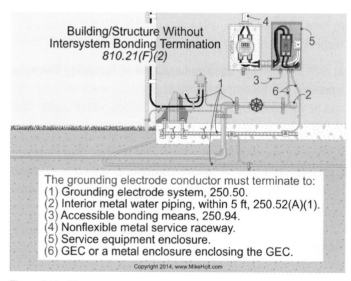

Figure 810–16

(1) Building grounding electrode system [250.50].

(2) Interior metal water piping system, within 5 ft from its point of entrance [250.52(A)(1)]. Figure 810–17

(3) Accessible means external to the building, as covered in 250.94.

(4) Nonflexible metallic service raceway.

(5) Service equipment enclosure.

(6) Grounding electrode conductor or the grounding electrode conductor metal enclosure.

(3) In Buildings Without a Grounding Means. The grounding electrode conductor for the antenna mast and antenna discharge unit must be connected to a grounding electrode as described in 250.52.

(G) Inside or Outside Building. The bonding conductor or grounding electrode conductor can be installed either inside or outside the building.

(H) Size. The bonding conductor or grounding electrode conductor must not be smaller than 10 AWG copper or 17 AWG copper-clad steel or bronze.

Author's Comment:

■ Copper-clad steel or bronze wire (17 AWG) is often molded into the jacket of the coaxial cable to simplify the grounding of the lead-in conductor from an outdoor antenna to the discharge unit [810.21(F)].

(J) Bonding of Electrodes. If a ground rod is installed to serve as the grounding electrode for the radio and television equipment, it must be connected to the building's power grounding electrode system with a minimum 6 AWG conductor. Figure 810–18

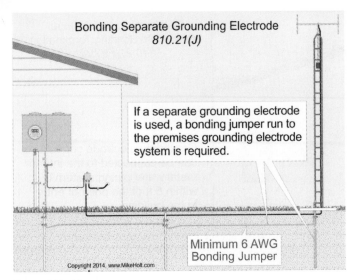

Figure 810–18

(K) Electrode Connection. Termination of the bonding conductor or grounding electrode conductor must be by exothermic welding, listed lugs, listed pressure connectors, or listed clamps. Grounding fittings that are concrete-encased or buried in the earth must be listed for direct burial [250.70].

Part III. Amateur and Citizen Band Transmitting and Receiving Antenna Systems

810.51 Other Sections

Antenna systems for amateur and citizen band transmitting and receiving stations must also comply with the following requirements:

Support of Lead-In Cables. Antennas and lead-in conductors must be securely supported, and the lead-in conductors must be securely attached to the antenna [810.12].

Avoid Contact with Conductors of Other Systems. Outdoor antennas and lead-in conductors must be kept at least 2 ft from exposed electric power conductors to avoid the possibility of accidental contact [810.13].

Metal Antenna Supports—Grounding. Outdoor masts and metal structures that support antennas must be grounded in accordance with 810.21 [810.15].

810.54 Clearance on Building

Antenna lead-in conductors must be firmly mounted at least 3 in. away from the surface of the building.

810.57 Antenna Discharge Units

Each lead-in conductor from an outdoor antenna must be provided with a listed antenna discharge unit or other suitable means that drain static charges from the antenna system.

Ex 1: If protected by a continuous metallic shield that's grounded in accordance with 810.58.

Ex 2: If the antenna is grounded in accordance with 810.58.

810.58 Bonding Conductor or Grounding Electrode Conductors

(A) Other Sections. The antenna mast [810.15] and antenna discharge unit [810.57] must be grounded as specified in 810.21.

(B) Size of Protective Bonding Conductor or Grounding Electrode Conductor. The bonding conductor or grounding electrode conductor must be the same size as the lead-in conductors, but not smaller than 10 AWG copper, bronze, or copper-clad steel.

(C) Size of Operating Bonding Conductor or Grounding Electrode Conductor. The operating bonding conductor or grounding electrode conductor for transmitting stations must not be smaller than 14 AWG copper or its equivalent.

ARTICLE 810 PRACTICE QUESTIONS

Please use the 2014 *Code* book to answer the following questions.

1. Article _____ contains the installation requirements for the wiring of television and radio receiving equipment, such as digital satellite receiving equipment for television signals and amateur/citizen band radio equipment antennas.

   (a) 680
   (b) 700
   (c) 810
   (d) 840

2. Outdoor antennas and lead-in conductors shall be securely supported and the lead-in conductors shall be securely attached to the antenna, but they shall not be attached to the electric service mast.

   (a) True
   (b) False

3. Underground antenna conductors for radio and television receiving equipment shall be separated at least _____ from any light, power, or Class 1 circuit conductors.

   (a) 12 in.
   (b) 18 in.
   (c) 5 ft
   (d) 6 ft

4. Indoor antenna and lead-in conductors for radio and television receiving equipment shall be separated by at least _____ from conductors of any electric light, power, or Class 1 circuit conductors, unless otherwise permitted.

   (a) 2 in.
   (b) 12 in.
   (c) 18 in.
   (d) 6 ft

5. Indoor antenna lead-in conductors for radio and television receiving equipment can be in the same enclosure with conductors of other wiring systems where separated by an effective permanently installed barrier.

   (a) True
   (b) False

6. Antenna discharge units shall be located outside the building only.

   (a) True
   (b) False

7. The grounding electrode conductor for an antenna mast shall be _____ protected where subject to physical damage.

   (a) electrically
   (b) mechanically
   (c) arc-fault
   (d) none of these

8. Radio and television receiving antenna systems must have bonding or grounding electrode conductors that are _____.

    (a) copper or other corrosion-resistant conductive material
    (b) insulated, covered, or bare
    (c) securely fastened in place and protected where subject to physical damage
    (d) all of these

9. The bonding conductor or grounding electrode conductor for a radio/television antenna system must be protected where subject to physical damage, and where installed in a metal raceway, both ends of the raceway must be bonded to the _____ conductor.

    (a) contained
    (b) grounded
    (c) ungrounded
    (d) b or c

10. The bonding conductor or grounding electrode conductor for an antenna mast or antenna discharge unit shall be run to the grounding electrode in as straight a line as practicable.

    (a) True
    (b) False

11. If the building or structure served has an intersystem bonding termination, the bonding conductor for an antenna mast shall be connected to the intersystem bonding termination.

    (a) True
    (b) False

12. The grounding conductor for an antenna mast or antenna discharge unit, if copper, shall not be smaller than 10 AWG.

    (a) True
    (b) False

13. If a separate grounding electrode is installed for the radio and television equipment, it shall be bonded to the building's electrical power grounding electrode system with a bonding jumper not smaller than _____ AWG.

    (a) 10
    (b) 8
    (c) 6
    (d) 1/0

14. Antenna conductors for amateur transmitting stations attached to buildings shall be firmly mounted at least _____ in. clear of the surface of the building on nonabsorbent insulating supports.

    (a) 1
    (b) 2
    (c) 3
    (d) 4

COMMUNITY ANTENNA TELEVISION (CATV) AND RADIO DISTRIBUTION SYSTEMS

Introduction to Article 820—Community Antenna Television (CATV) and Radio Distribution Systems

This article focuses on the distribution of television and radio signals within a facility or on a property via cable, rather than their transmission or reception via antenna. These signals are limited energy, but they're high frequency.

- As with Article 800, you must determine the "point of entrance" for these circuits.
- Ground the incoming coaxial cable as close as practicable to the point of entrance.
- If coaxial cables are located above a suspended ceiling, route and support them to allow access via ceiling panel removal.
- Clearances are critical, and Article 820 contains detailed clearance requirements. For example, it requires at least 6 ft of clearance between coaxial cable and lightning conductors.
- If the building or structure has an intersystem bonding termination, the bonding conductor must be connected to it.
- If you use a separate grounding electrode, you must run a bonding jumper to the power grounding system.

Author's Comment:

■ For Articles 800, 810, and 820, the difference between a "bonding conductor" and a "grounding electrode conductor" is where they terminate. The bonding conductor terminates at the intersystem bonding termination; the grounding electrode connects to the power grounding electrode system [250.50].

Part I. General

820.1 Scope

Article 820 covers the installation of coaxial cables for distributing high-frequency signals typically employed in community antenna television (CATV) systems. Figure 820–1

Note: The *NEC* installation requirements don't apply to communications utility equipment, such as CATV located outdoors or in building spaces under the exclusive control of the communications utility [90.2(B)(4)].

Author's Comment:

■ Coaxial cables that connect antennas to television and radio receiving equipment [810.3] and community television systems [810.4] must be installed in accordance with this article. Figure 820–2

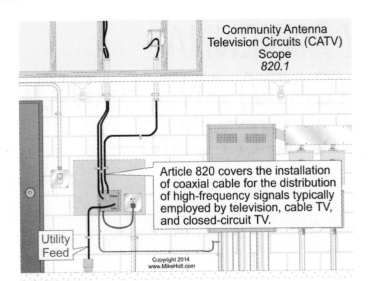

Figure 820–1

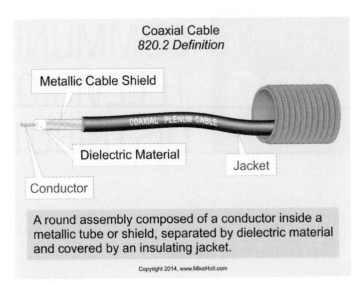

Figure 820–3

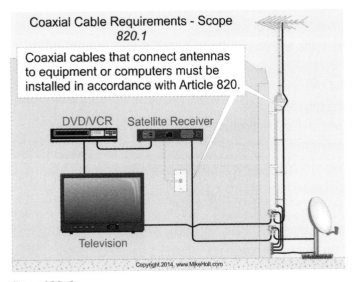

Figure 820–2

Point of Entrance. The point within a building where the coaxial cable emerges from an external wall, from a concrete floor slab, from rigid metal conduit, or intermediate metal conduit. Figure 820–4

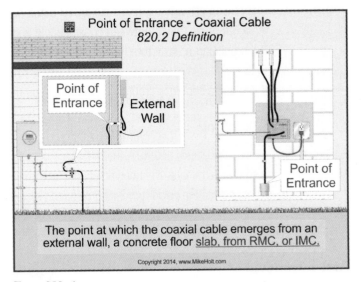

Figure 820–4

820.2 Definitions

Abandoned Coaxial Cable. A cable that isn't terminated to equipment and not identified for future use with a tag.

Coaxial Cable. A round assembly composed of a conductor inside a metallic tube or shield, separated by dielectric material, and usually covered by an insulating jacket. Figure 820–3

820.15 Power Limitations

Coaxial cable is permitted to deliver power at a maximum of 60V to equipment that's directly associated with the radio frequency distribution system.

820.21 Access to Electrical Equipment Behind Panels Designed to Allow Access

Access to equipment must not be prohibited by an accumulation of coaxial cables that prevent the removal of suspended-ceiling panels. Figure 820–5

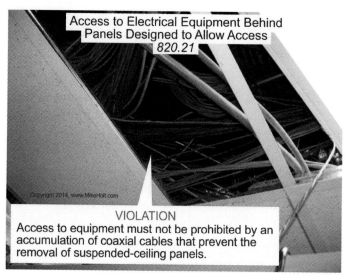

VIOLATION
Access to equipment must not be prohibited by an accumulation of coaxial cables that prevent the removal of suspended-ceiling panels.

Figure 820–5

820.24 Mechanical Execution of Work

Equipment and coaxial cabling must be installed in a neat and work-manlike manner. Exposed coaxial cables must be supported by the structural components of the building so that the coaxial cable won't be damaged by normal building use. Coaxial cables must be secured by straps, staples, cable ties, hangers, or similar fittings designed and installed so as not to damage the coaxial cable. Figure 820–6

Raceways that contain coaxial cables must be securely fastened in place. Ceiling-support wires or the ceiling grid must not be used to support raceways or coaxial cables [300.11]. Figure 820–7

Author's Comment:

■ Raceways and coaxial cables can be supported by independent support wires attached to the suspended ceiling in accordance with 300.11(A).

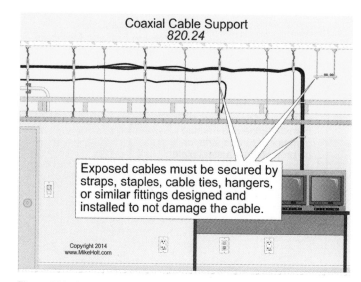

Coaxial Cable Support
820.24

Exposed cables must be secured by straps, staples, cable ties, hangers, or similar fittings designed and installed to not damage the cable.

Figure 820–6

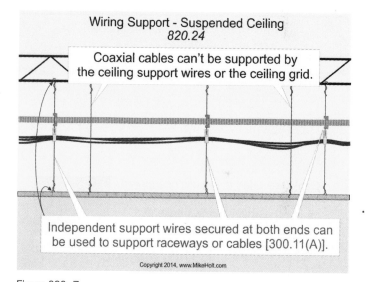

Wiring Support - Suspended Ceiling
820.24

Coaxial cables can't be supported by the ceiling support wires or the ceiling grid.

Independent support wires secured at both ends can be used to support raceways or cables [300.11(A)].

Figure 820–7

Coaxial cables installed through or parallel to framing members or furring strips must be protected where they're likely to be penetrated by nails or screws, by installing the coaxial cables so they aren't less than 1¼ in. from the nearest edge of the framing member or furring strips, or by protecting the coaxial cable with a ¹⁄₁₆ in. thick steel plate or the equivalent [300.4(D)]. Figure 820–8

Cable ties used to secure or support coaxial cables in plenums must be listed for use in plenums. Figure 820–9

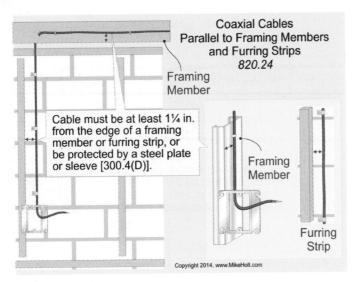

Figure 820–8

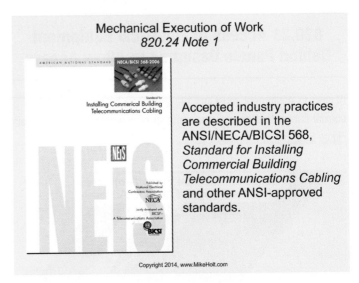

Figure 820–10

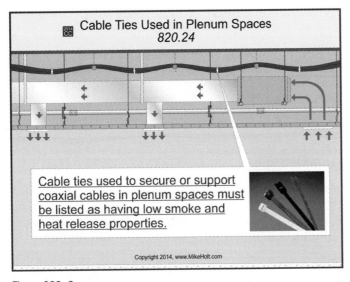

Figure 820–9

Note 1: Accepted industry practices are described in ANSI/NECA/BICSI 568, *Standard for Installing Commercial Building Telecommunications Cabling*, ANSI/TIA/EIA 568-B, *Part 1, General Requirements Commercial Building Telecommunications Cabling Standard*, ANSI/TIA 569-B, *Commercial Building Standard for Telecommunications Pathways and Spaces*, ANSI/TIA 570-B, *Residential Telecommunications Infrastructure*, and other ANSI-approved standards. Figure 820–10

Author's Comment:

■ For more information about these standards, visit www. NECA-NEIS.org.

Note 2: See 4.3.11.2.6.5 and 4.3.11.5.5.6 of NFPA 90A, *Standard for the Installation of Air-Conditioning and Ventilating Systems*, for discrete combustible components installed in accordance with 300.22(C).

820.25 Abandoned Cable

To limit the spread of fire or products of combustion within a building, the accessible portion of coaxial cable that isn't terminated at equipment, and not identified for future use with a tag, must be removed [820.2]. Figure 820–11

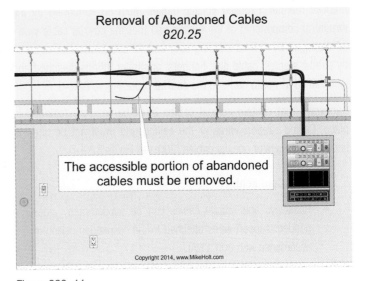

Figure 820–11

Cables identified for future use must be with a tag that can withstand the environment involved. Figure 820–12

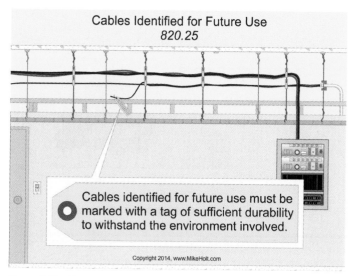

Figure 820–12

Author's Comment:

- Cables installed in concealed raceways aren't considered "accessible"; therefore, they're not required to be removed.

820.26 Spread of Fire or Products of Combustion

Coaxial cables and communications raceways and equipment must be installed in such a way that the spread of fire or products of combustion won't be substantially increased. Openings in fire-rated walls, floors, and ceilings for coaxial cables and communications raceways must be firestopped using methods approved by the authority having jurisdiction to maintain the fire-resistance-rating of the fire-rated assembly. Figure 820–13

Author's Comment:

- Firestop material is listed for the specific types of wiring methods and construction structures.

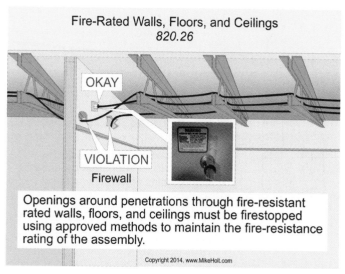

Figure 820–13

Note: Directories of electrical construction materials published by qualified testing laboratories contain listing and installation restrictions necessary to maintain the fire-resistive rating of assemblies. For example, outlet boxes must have a horizontal separation not less than 24 in. when installed in a fire-rated assembly, unless an outlet box is listed for closer spacing or protected by fire-resistant "putty pads" in accordance with manufacturer's instructions.

Part II. Coaxial Cables Outside and Entering Buildings

820.44 Supports

(C) On Mast. Overhead (aerial) coaxial cables are permitted to be attached to an above-the-roof raceway mast that does not enclose or support conductors of electric light or power circuits. Figure 820–14

(E) On Buildings. Where attached to buildings, coaxial cables must be securely fastened in such a manner that they'll be separated from other conductors.

(1) Electric Light or Power. Coaxial cable must have a separation of at least 4 in. from electric light, power, Class 1, or non–power-limited fire alarm circuit conductors not in raceway or cable.

(3) Lightning Conductors. Where practicable, a separation of at least 6 ft must be maintained between any coaxial cable and lightning conductors. Figure 820–15

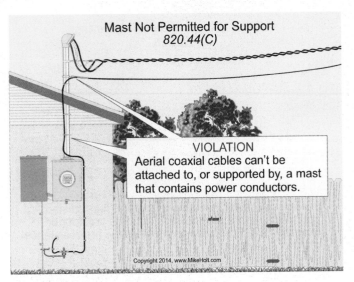

Figure 820–14

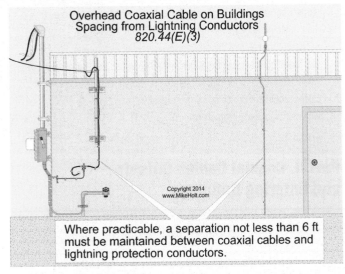

Figure 820–15

820.47 Underground Coaxial Cables Entering Buildings

(A) Underground Systems with Electric Light, Power, Class 1, or Non–Power-Limited Fire Alarm Circuit Conductors. Underground coaxial cables in a duct, pedestal, handhole enclosure, or manhole that contains electric light, power, or Class 1 or non–power-limited fire alarm circuit conductors must be in a section permanently separated from such conductors by means of a suitable barrier.

(B) Direct-Buried Cables and Raceways. Direct-buried coaxial cable must be separated at least 12 in. from conductors of any light or power. Figure 820–16

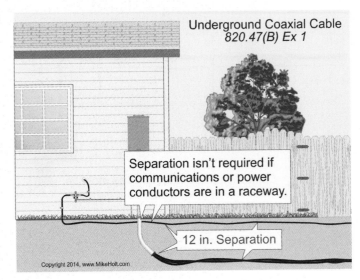

Figure 820–16

Ex 2: Where electric light or power conductors or coaxial cables are installed in a Chapter 3 wiring method.

820.48 Unlisted Cables and Raceways Entering Building

Unlisted coaxial cable is permitted in building spaces, other than plenums, if the length of the coaxial cable within the building from its point of entrance doesn't exceed 50 ft and the coaxial cable terminates at a grounding block. Figure 820–17

820.49 Metallic Entrance Conduit Grounding

Rigid metal conduit (RMC) or intermediate metal conduit (IMC) containing entrance coaxial cable must be connected to a grounding electrode in accordance with 820.100(B). Figure 820–18

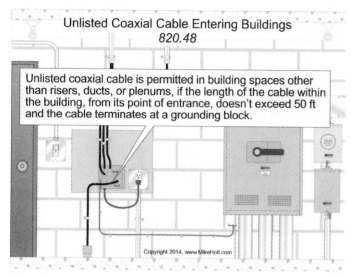

Figure 820–17

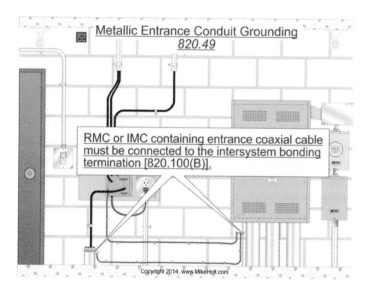

Figure 820–18

Part III. Protection

820.93 Grounding of the Outer Conductive Shield of Coaxial Cables

(A) Coaxial CATV Cables Entering Building. Coaxial CATV cables supplied to a building must have the metallic sheath members bonded/grounded as close as practicable to the point of entrance in accordance with 820.100. Figure 820–19

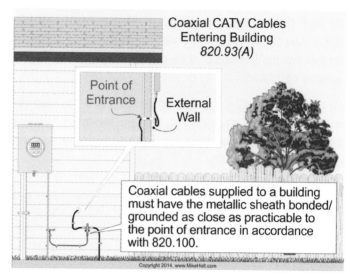

Figure 820–19

Note: Limiting the length of the bonding conductor or grounding electrode conductor helps limit damage to equipment because of a potential (voltage) difference between communications equipment and other systems during lightning events [820.100(A)(4)].

Part IV. Grounding Methods

820.100 Bonding and Grounding Methods

The outer conductive shield of a coaxial cable must be bonded or grounded in accordance with the following:

Ex: Coaxial cable confined within the premises and isolated from the outside cable plant can be grounded by a connection to an equipment grounding conductor as described in 250.118. Connecting to an equipment grounding conductor through a grounded receptacle using a dedicated bonding jumper and a permanently connected listed device is permitted. Use of a cord and plug for the connection to an equipment grounding conductor isn't permitted.

(A) Bonding Conductor or Grounding Electrode Conductor.

(1) Insulation. The bonding conductor or grounding electrode conductor must be listed and can be insulated, covered, or bare.

(2) Material. The bonding conductor or grounding electrode conductor must be copper or other corrosion-resistant conductive material, stranded or solid.

(3) Size. The bonding conductor or grounding electrode conductor must not be smaller than 14 AWG with a current-carrying capacity of not less than the outer sheath of the coaxial cable, but not required to be larger than 6 AWG.

(4) Length. The bonding conductor or grounding electrode conductor must be as short as practicable. For one- and two-family dwellings, the bonding conductor or grounding electrode conductor must not exceed 20 ft. Figure 820–20

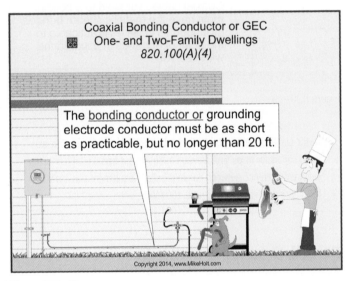

Figure 820–20

Note: Limiting the length of the bonding conductor or grounding electrode conductor at other than dwelling units will help to reduce potential (voltage) differences between the building's power and CATV systems during lightning events.

Ex: If it's not practicable to limit the coaxial bonding conductor or grounding electrode conductor to 20 ft in length for one- and two-family dwellings, a separate rod not less than 8 ft long [250.52(A)(5)], with fittings suitable for the application [250.70] must be installed. The additional rod must be bonded to the power grounding electrode system with a minimum 6 AWG conductor [820.100(D)]. Figure 820–21

(5) Run in Straight Line. The bonding conductor or grounding electrode conductor to the electrode must be run in as straight a line as practicable.

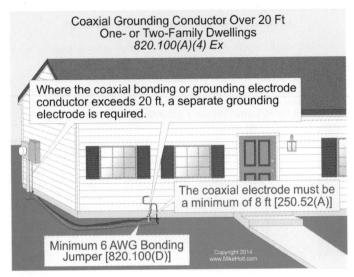

Figure 820–21

Author's Comment:

■ Lightning doesn't like to travel around corners or through loops, which is why the bonding conductor or grounding electrode conductor must be run as straight as practicable.

(6) Physical Protection. The bonding conductor or grounding electrode conductor must be mechanically protected where subject to physical damage, and where installed in a metal raceway both ends of the raceway must be bonded to the bonding conductor or grounding electrode conductor. Figure 820–22

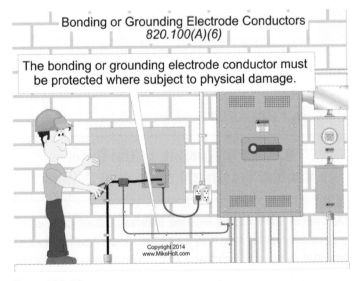

Figure 820–22

Author's Comment:

- Installing the bonding conductor in PVC conduit is a better practice.

(B) Electrode. The bonding conductor or grounding electrode conductor must be connected in accordance with (B)(1), (B)(2), or (B)(3).

(1) Buildings With an Intersystem Bonding Termination. The bonding conductor or grounding electrode conductor for the CATV system must terminate to the intersystem bonding termination as required by 250.94. Figure 820–23

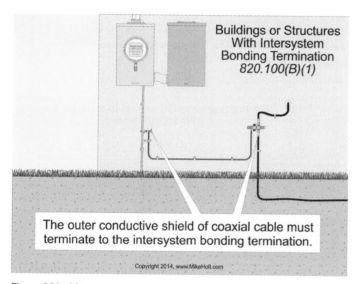

Figure 820–23

Note: According to the Article 100 definition, an "Intersystem Bonding Termination" is a device that provides a means to connect bonding conductors for communications systems to the grounding electrode system, in accordance with 250.94. Figure 820–24

Author's Comment:

- Bonding all systems to the intersystem bonding termination helps reduce induced potential (voltage) differences between the power and the radio and television systems during lightning events.

(2) In Buildings Without Intersystem Bonding Termination. At existing structures, the bonding conductor or grounding electrode conductor must terminate to the nearest accessible: Figure 820–25

(1) Building grounding electrode system [250.50].

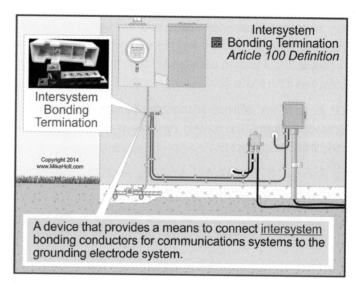

Figure 820–24

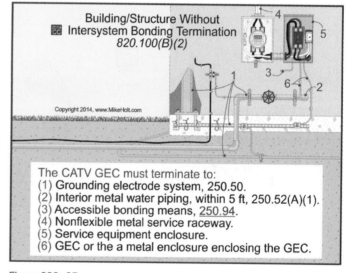

Figure 820–25

(2) Interior metal water piping system, within 5 ft from its point of entrance [250.52(A)(1)].

(3) Accessible means external to the building, as covered in 250.94.

(4) Nonflexible metallic service raceway of the power service.

(5) Service equipment enclosure.

(6) Grounding electrode conductor or the grounding electrode conductor metal enclosure.

(7) The grounding electrode conductor or the grounding electrode of a remote building disconnecting means [250.32].

The intersystem bonding termination must be mounted on the fixed part of an enclosure so that it won't interfere with the opening of an enclosure door. A bonding device must not be mounted on a door or cover even if the door or cover is nonremovable.

(3) In Buildings Without Intersystem Bonding Termination or Grounding Means. The bonding conductor or grounding electrode conductor must connect to:

(1) Any one of the individual <u>grounding</u> electrodes described in 250.52(A)(1), (A)(2), (A)(3), (A)(4), or

(2) Any individual grounding electrodes described in 250.52(A)(5), 250.52(A)(7), and (A)(8). Figure 820–26

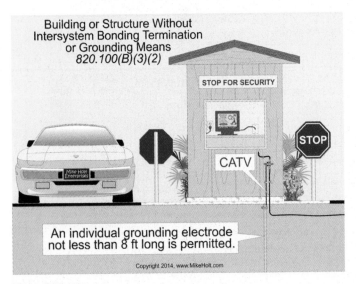

Figure 820–26

(C) Electrode Connection. Terminations to the grounding electrode must be by exothermic welding, listed lugs, listed pressure connectors, or clamps. Grounding fittings that are concrete-encased or buried in the earth must be listed for direct burial [250.70].

(D) Bonding of Electrodes. If a separate grounding electrode, such as a rod, is installed for the CATV system, it must be bonded to the building's power grounding electrode system with a minimum 6 AWG conductor. Figure 820–27

> **Note 2:** Bonding all systems to the intersystem bonding termination helps reduce induced potential (voltage) between the power and CATV system during lightning events. Figure 820–28

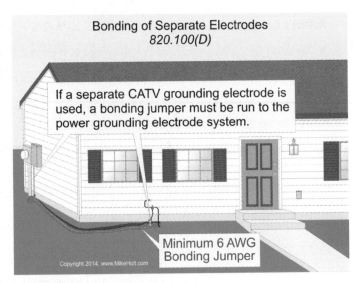

Figure 820–27

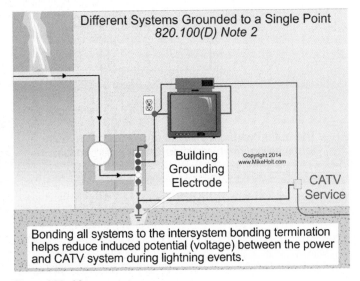

Figure 820–28

Part V. Installation Methods Within Buildings

820.110 Raceways <u>and Cable Routing Assemblies</u> for Coaxial Cables

(A) Types of Raceways.

(1) Chapter 3 Raceways. Coaxial cables can be installed in any Chapter 3 raceway and installed in accordance with the requirements of Chapter 3. Figure 820–29

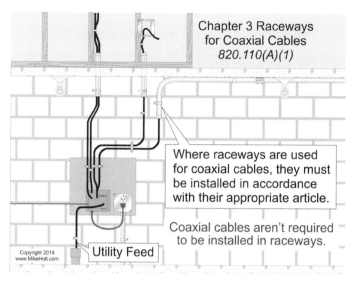

Figure 820–29

(2) Communications Raceways. Coaxial cables can be installed in listed communications <u>raceways</u> selected in accordance with the provisions of <u>800.110, 800.113, and</u> 820.113. If coaxial cables are installed in a listed communications <u>raceway</u>, the raceway must be installed in accordance with 362.24 through 362.56. Figure 820–30

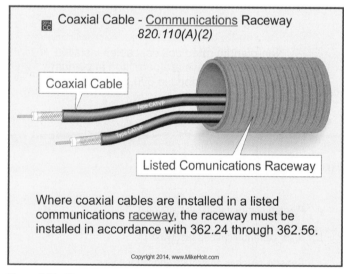

Figure 820–30

Author's Comment:

■ In other words, listed coaxial raceways must be installed in accordance with the following rules for ENT:

    ❑ 362.24 Bending radius

    ❑ 362.26 Maximum total bends between pull points, 360 degrees

    ❑ 362.28 Trimmed to remove rough edges

    ❑ 362.30 Supported every 3 ft, and within 3 ft of any enclosure

    ❑ 362.48 Joints between tubing, fittings, and boxes

■ A communications raceway is an enclosed channel of non-metallic materials designed for holding communications wire and cables, optical fiber cables and Class 2 and 3 circuits [Article 100]. Figure 820–31

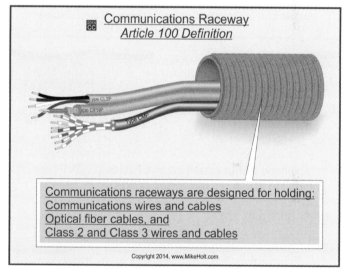

Figure 820–31

(B) Raceway Fill for Coaxial Cables. Raceway fill limitations of 300.17 don't apply to coaxial cables installed in a raceway.

(C) Cable Routing Assemblies. Coaxial cables can be installed in cable routing assemblies selected in accordance with 800.113. They must also be installed in accordance with the following:

(1) Horizontal Support. Where installed horizontally, cable routing assemblies must be supported every 3 ft, and at each end or joint, unless listed otherwise. The distance between supports can never exceed 10 ft.

(2) Vertical Support. Where installed vertically, cable routing assemblies must be supported every 4 ft, unless listed otherwise, and must not have more than one joint between supports.

820.113 Installation of Coaxial Cables

(A) Listing. Coaxial cables installed within buildings must be listed.

Ex: Unless the length of the cable from its point of entrance, doesn't exceed 50 ft as permitted by 820.48.

(C) Plenum Spaces.

(1) Plenum Rated Cables. Exposed plenum rated coaxial cables (CATVP) are permitted in plenum spaces as described in 300.22(C): Figure 820–32

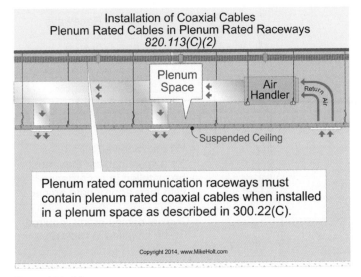

Installation of Coaxial Cables
Plenum Rated Cables in Plenum Rated Raceways
820.113(C)(2)

Plenum rated communication raceways must contain plenum rated coaxial cables when installed in a plenum space as described in 300.22(C).

Figure 820–33

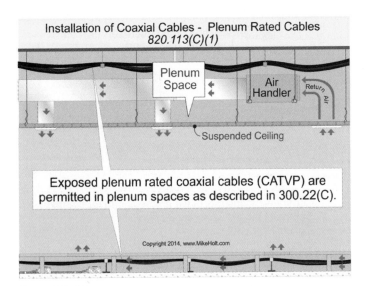

Installation of Coaxial Cables - Plenum Rated Cables
820.113(C)(1)

Exposed plenum rated coaxial cables (CATVP) are permitted in plenum spaces as described in 300.22(C).

Figure 820–32

(2) Plenum Rated Cable in Plenum Rated Raceways. Plenum communications raceways must contain plenum rated cables in a plenum space as described in 300.22(C). Figure 820–33

(4) Non-Plenum Rated Cables. Non-plenum rated coaxial cables installed in metal raceways are permitted in plenum spaces as described in 300.22(C). Figure 820–34

(H) Cable Trays. The following cables can be supported by cable trays:

(1) Types CATVP, CATVR, and CATV cables

(2) Types CATVP, CATVR, and CATV cables installed in:

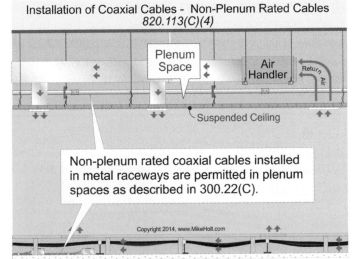

Installation of Coaxial Cables - Non-Plenum Rated Cables
820.113(C)(4)

Non-plenum rated coaxial cables installed in metal raceways are permitted in plenum spaces as described in 300.22(C).

Figure 820–34

a. Plenum communications raceways

b. Riser communications raceways

c. General-purpose communications raceways

(J) Other Building Locations. The following cables can be installed in building locations other than the locations covered in 820.113(B) through (I):

(1) Types CATVP, CATVR, and CATV cables

(2) A maximum of 10 ft of exposed Type CATVX cables in nonconcealed spaces

(3) Types CATVP, CATVR, and CATV cables installed in:

    a. Plenum communications <u>raceways</u>

    <u>b.</u> <u>Plenum cable routing assemblies</u>

    <u>c.</u> Riser communications <u>raceways</u>

    d. Riser cable routing assemblies

    <u>e.</u> General-purpose communications <u>raceways</u>

    <u>f.</u> General-purpose cable routing <u>assemblies</u>

(4) Types CATVP, CATVR, CATV, and Type CATVX cables installed in a Chapter 3 raceway

(K) One- and Two-Family and Multifamily Dwellings. The following cables and cable routing assemblies can be installed in one- and two-family and multifamily dwellings in locations other than the locations covered in 820.113(B) through (I):

(1) Types CATVP, CATVR, CATV cables

(2) Type CATVX cable less than 0.375 in. in diameter

(3) Types CATVP, CATVR, and CATV cables installed in:

    a. Plenum communications <u>raceways</u>

    <u>b.</u> <u>Plenum cable routing assemblies</u>

    <u>c.</u> Riser communications <u>raceways</u>

    d. Riser cable routing assemblies

    <u>e.</u> General-purpose communications <u>raceways</u>

    <u>f.</u> General-purpose cable routing <u>assemblies</u>

820.133 Installation of Coaxial Cables and Equipment

(A) Separation from Other Conductors.

(1) In Raceways, <u>Cable</u> Trays, Boxes, <u>Cable Routing Assemblies, and Enclosures</u>.

(a) With Optical Fiber Cables. Coaxial cables can be in the same raceway, <u>box</u>, cable tray, cable routing assembly or <u>enclosure</u> with jacketed cables of any of the following: Figure 820–35

(1) Optical fiber cables in accordance with Parts I and <u>V</u> of Article 770.

(2) Communications circuits in compliance with Parts I and <u>V</u> of Article 800.

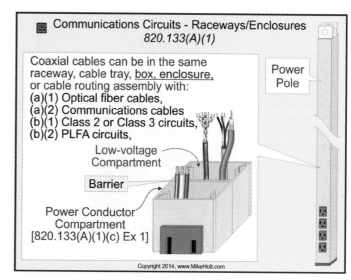

Figure 820–35

(b) With Other Circuits. Coaxial cables can be in the same raceway, cable tray, <u>box, cable routing assembly, or enclosure</u> with jacketed cables of any of the following:

(1) Class 2 and Class 3 circuits in compliance with <u>Article 645 or</u> Parts I and III of Article 725.

(2) Power-limited fire alarm circuits in compliance with Parts I and III of Article 760.

(c) Electric Light, Power, Class 1, Nonpower-Limited Fire Alarm, and Medium-Power Network-Powered Broadband Communications Circuits. Coaxial cable must not be placed in any raceway, compartment, outlet box, junction box, or other enclosures with conductors of electric light, power, Class 1, nonpower-limited fire alarm, or medium-power network-powered broadband communications circuits.

Ex 1: Coaxial cables are permitted with conductors of electric power and Class 1 circuits, where separated by a permanent barrier or listed divider. Figure 820–36

Author's Comment:

- Separation is required to prevent a fire or shock hazard that can occur from a short between the higher-voltage circuits and the coaxial cable.

Ex 2: Coaxial cables can be mixed in enclosures other than raceways or cables with power conductors if the power circuit conductors are only introduced to supply power to coaxial cable system distribution equipment. The power circuit conductors must be separated at least ¼ in. from the coaxial cables.

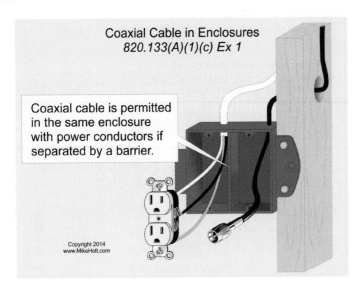

Figure 820–36

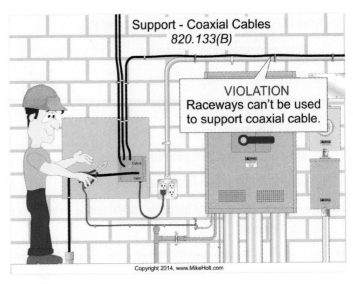

Figure 820–38

(2) Other Applications. Coaxial cables must maintain 2 in. of separation from electric power or Class 1 circuit conductors.

Ex 1: Separation isn't required if electric power or conductors are in a raceway or in metal-sheathed, metal-clad, nonmetallic-sheathed, or underground feeder cables, or coaxial cables are in a raceway. Figure 820–37

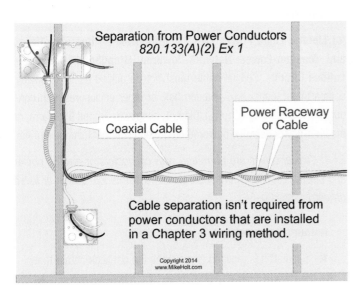

Figure 820–37

(B) Support of Cables. Coaxial cables aren't permitted to be strapped, taped, or attached to the exterior of any raceway as a means of support. Figure 820–38

Ex: Overhead (aerial) spans of coaxial cables can be attached to a raceway-type mast intended for the attachment and support of such conductors. Figure 820–39

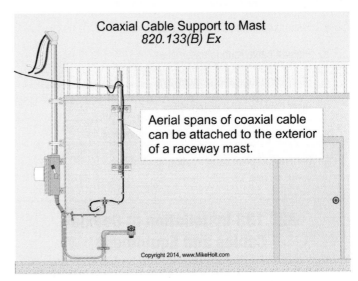

Figure 820–39

820.154 Applications of Coaxial Cables

Listed coaxial cables can be installed as indicated in Table 820.154(a) as limited by 820.110 and 820.113, and cable substitutions in accordance with Table 820.154(b). Figure 820–40

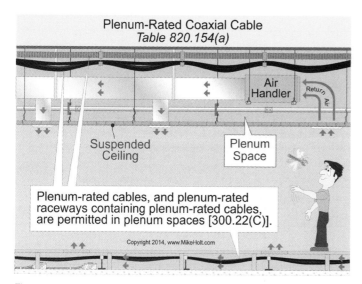

Figure 820–40

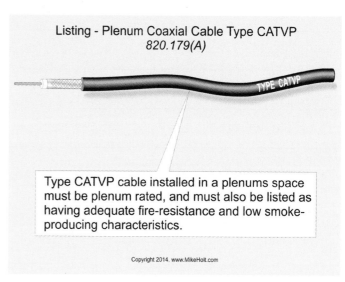

Figure 820–41

Part VI. Listing Requirements

820.179 Listing and Marking of Coaxial Cables

Coaxial cables must be listed in accordance with 820.179(A) through (D) and marked in accordance with Table 820.179.

(A) Type CATVP. Type CATVP plenum cable is listed as being suitable for use in plenum space. Figure 820–41

ARTICLE 820 PRACTICE QUESTIONS

Please use the 2014 *Code* book to answer the following questions.

1. Article _____ covers the installation of coaxial cables for distributing radio frequency signals typically employed in community antenna television (CATV) systems.

   (a) 300
   (b) 430
   (c) 800
   (d) 820

2. CATV cable not terminated at equipment other than a coaxial cable connector and not identified for future use with a tag is considered abandoned.

   (a) True
   (b) False

3. Coaxial cable is a cylindrical assembly composed of a conductor centered inside a metallic tube or shield, separated by a(n) _____ material and usually covered by an insulating jacket.

   (a) insulating
   (b) conductive
   (c) isolating
   (d) dielectric

4. The point of entrance of a CATV coaxial cable is the point _____ at which the coaxial cable emerges from an external wall, from a concrete floor slab, from rigid metal conduit (RMC). or from intermediate metal conduit (IMC).

   (a) outside a building
   (b) within a building
   (c) on the building
   (d) none of these

5. CATV coaxial cable can deliver power to equipment that is directly associated with the radio frequency distribution system if the voltage is not over _____ and if the current supply is from a transformer or other power-limiting device.

   (a) 60V
   (b) 120V
   (c) 180V
   (d) 270V

6. Access to electrical equipment shall not be denied by an accumulation of CATV coaxial cables that _____ removal of suspended-ceiling panels.

   (a) prevents
   (b) hinders
   (c) blocks
   (d) require

7. CATV coaxial cables installed _____ on the surface of ceilings and walls shall be supported by the building structure in such a manner that the cables will not be damaged by normal building use.

   (a) exposed
   (b) concealed
   (c) hidden
   (d) a and b

8. Exposed CATV cables shall be secured by hardware such as straps, staples, cable ties, hangers, or similar fittings designed and installed so as not to damage the cables.

   (a) True
   (b) False

9. Accessible portions of abandoned CATV cable shall be removed unless tagged for future use.

(a) True
(b) False

10. Openings around penetrations of CATV coaxial cables and communications raceways through fire-resistant–rated walls, partitions, floors, or ceilings shall be _____ using approved methods to maintain the fire-resistance rating.

(a) closed
(b) opened
(c) draft stopped
(d) firestopped

11. Community antenna television and radio system coaxial cables shall not be required to be listed and marked where the length of the cable within the building, measured from its point of entrance, does not exceed _____ ft, the cable enters the building from the outside and the cable is terminated at a grounding block.

(a) 25
(b) 30
(c) 50
(d) 100

12. The outer conductive shield of a CATV coaxial cable entering a building shall be grounded as close to the point of entrance as practicable.

(a) True
(b) False

13. The conductor used to ground the outer cover of a CATV coaxial cable shall be permitted to be _____.

(a) insulated
(b) 14 AWG minimum
(c) bare
(d) all of these

14. In one- and two-family dwellings, the grounding electrode conductor for CATV shall be as short as practicable, not to exceed _____ in length.

(a) 5 ft
(b) 8 ft
(c) 10 ft
(d) 20 ft

15. In one- and two-family dwellings where it is not practicable to achieve an overall maximum bonding conductor or equipment grounding conductor length of _____ for CATV, a separate grounding electrode as specified in 250.52(A)(5), (A)(6), or (A)(7) shall be used.

(a) 5 ft
(b) 8 ft
(c) 10 ft
(d) 20 ft

16. Limiting the length of the primary protector grounding conductors for community antenna television and radio systems reduces voltages that may develop between the building's _____ and communications systems during lightning events.

(a) power
(b) fire alarm
(c) lighting
(d) lightning protection

17. Bonding conductors and grounding electrode conductors shall be _____ where exposed to physical damage.

(a) electrically
(b) arc-fault
(c) protected
(d) none of these

18. A bonding jumper not smaller than _____ copper or equivalent shall be connected between the CATV system's grounding electrode and the power grounding electrode system at the building or structure served where separate electrodes are used.

(a) 12 AWG
(b) 8 AWG
(c) 6 AWG
(d) 4 AWG

19. Coaxial cables can be installed in any Chapter 3 raceway in accordance with the requirements of Chapter 3.

    (a) True
    (b) False

20. Coaxial cables can be installed in listed communications raceways. If coaxial cables are installed in a listed communications nonmetallic raceway, the raceway must be installed in accordance with 362.24 through 362.56, where the requirements applicable to ENT apply.

    (a) True
    (b) False

21. Raceway fill limitations of 300.17 apply to coaxial cables installed in a raceway.

    (a) True
    (b) False

22. Coaxial cables installed in buildings for CATV shall be listed except for the first 50 ft that enters a building in accordance with 820.48.

    (a) True
    (b) False

23. Coaxial cables used for CATV systems shall not be strapped, taped, or attached by any means to the exterior of any _____ as a means of support.

    (a) conduit
    (b) raceway
    (c) raceway-type mast intended for overhead spans of such cables
    (d) a or b

Mike Holt's Understanding 2014 NEC Requirements for Limited Energy & Communications Systems

FINAL EXAM FOR LIMITED ENERGY & COMMUNICATIONS SYSTEMS

Please use the 2014 *Code* book to answer the following questions.

1. Optical fiber cables not terminated at equipment, and not identified for future use with a tag are considered abandoned.

   (a) True
   (b) False

2. Unlisted conductive and nonconductive outside plant optical fiber cables shall be permitted to be installed in locations other than risers, ducts used for environmental air, plenums used for environmental air, and other spaces used for environmental air, where the length of the cable within the building, measured from its point of entrance, does not exceed _____ ft and the cable enters the building from the outside and is terminated in an enclosure.

   (a) 25
   (b) 50
   (c) 75
   (d) 100

3. Access to electrical equipment shall not be denied by an accumulation of communications _____ that prevents the removal of suspended-ceiling panels.

   (a) wires
   (b) cables
   (c) ductwork
   (d) a and b

4. In one- and two-family dwellings where it is not practicable to achieve an overall maximum primary protector grounding electrode conductor length of 20 ft, a separate ground rod not less than _____ ft shall be driven and it shall be connected to the power grounding electrode system with a 6 AWG conductor.

   (a) 5
   (b) 8
   (c) 10
   (d) 20

5. Limiting the length of the primary protector grounding conductors for communications circuits helps to reduce voltage between the building's _____ and communications systems during lightning events.

   (a) power
   (b) fire alarm
   (c) lighting
   (d) lightning protection

6. Optical fiber cables shall not be _____ to the exterior of any conduit or raceway as a means of support.

   (a) strapped
   (b) taped
   (c) attached
   (d) all of these

7. The outer conductive shield of a CATV coaxial cable entering a building shall be grounded as close to the point of entrance as practicable.

   (a) True
   (b) False

8. Conductors of Class 2 and Class 3 circuits shall not be placed in any enclosure, raceway, cable, or similar fittings with conductors of Class 1 or electric light or power conductors, unless _____.

   (a) insulated for the maximum voltage present
   (b) totally comprised of aluminum conductors
   (c) separated by a barrier
   (d) all of these

9. The power source for a Class 2 circuit shall be _____.

   (a) a listed Class 2 transformer
   (b) a listed Class 2 power supply
   (c) other listed equipment marked to identify the Class 2 power source
   (d) any of these

10. Cables and conductors of two or more power-limited fire alarm circuits can be installed in the same cable, enclosure, cable tray, raceway, or cable routing assembly.

    (a) True
    (b) False

11. Cables and conductors of Class 2 and Class 3 circuits _____ be placed with conductors of electric light, power, Class 1, non-power-limited fire alarm circuits, and medium power network-powered broadband communications circuits.

    (a) shall be permitted to
    (b) shall not
    (c) shall
    (d) none of these

12. Coaxial cable is a cylindrical assembly composed of a conductor centered inside a metallic tube or shield, separated by a(n) _____ material and usually covered by an insulating jacket.

    (a) insulating
    (b) conductive
    (c) isolating
    (d) dielectric

13. The bonding conductor or grounding electrode conductor for a radio/television antenna system must be protected where subject to physical damage, and where installed in a metal raceway, both ends of the raceway must be bonded to the _____ conductor.

    (a) contained
    (b) grounded
    (c) ungrounded
    (d) b or c

14. Antenna conductors for amateur transmitting stations attached to buildings shall be firmly mounted at least _____ in. clear of the surface of the building on nonabsorbent insulating supports.

    (a) 1
    (b) 2
    (c) 3
    (d) 4

15. Power-limited fire alarm cables can be supported by strapping, taping, or attaching to the exterior of a conduit or raceway.

    (a) True
    (b) False

16. Accepted industry practices for optical fiber installations are described in _____.

    (a) ANSI/NECA/BICSI 568, *Standard for Installing Commercial Building Telecommunications Cabling*
    (b) ANSI/NECA/FOA 301, *Standard for Installing and Testing Fiber Optic Cables*
    (c) other ANSI-approved installation standards
    (d) all of these

17. Remote-control circuits to safety-control equipment shall be classified as _____ if the failure of the equipment to operate introduces a direct fire or life hazard.

    (a) Class 1
    (b) Class 2
    (c) Class 3
    (d) Class I, Division 1

18. Raceway fill limitations of 300.17 apply to coaxial cables installed in a raceway.

    (a) True
    (b) False

19. The circuit that extends voice, audio, video, interactive services, telegraph (except radio), and outside wiring for fire alarm and burglar alarm from the communications utility to the customer's communications equipment up to and including equipment such as a telephone, fax machine or answering machine defines a "_____ circuit."

    (a) limited-energy
    (b) remote-signaling
    (c) power-limited
    (d) communications

20. Openings around penetrations of CATV coaxial cables and communications raceways through fire-resistant–rated walls, partitions, floors, or ceilings shall be _____ using approved methods to maintain the fire-resistance rating.

    (a) closed
    (b) opened
    (c) draft stopped
    (d) firestopped

21. Class 2 and Class 3 circuits installed _____ on the surface of ceilings and walls shall be supported by the building structure in such a manner that the cable will not be damaged by normal building use.

    (a) exposed
    (b) concealed
    (c) hidden
    (d) a and b

22. Optical fiber cables are not required to be listed and marked where the length of the cable within the building, measured from its point of entrance, does not exceed _____ ft and the cable enters the building from the outside and is terminated in an enclosure.

    (a) 25
    (b) 30
    (c) 50
    (d) 100

23. Coaxial cables can be installed in listed communications raceways. If coaxial cables are installed in a listed communications nonmetallic raceway, the raceway must be installed in accordance with 362.24 through 362.56, where the requirements applicable to ENT apply.

    (a) True
    (b) False

24. Due to its power limitations, a Class 2 circuit is considered safe from a fire initiation standpoint and provides acceptable protection from electric shock.

    (a) True
    (b) False

25. Accessible portions of abandoned optical fiber cable shall be removed.

    (a) True
    (b) False

26. If fire alarm conductors are installed in a raceway that is subjected to different temperatures, and where condensation is known to be a problem, the raceway must be filled with a material approved by the authority having jurisdiction that will prevent the circulation of warm air to a colder section of the raceway. An explosionproof seal _____.

    (a) is required for this purpose
    (b) has been proven effective for this purpose
    (c) isn't required for this purpose
    (d) is the only method of doing this

27. The fire alarm circuit disconnecting means for a power-limited fire alarm system must _____.

    (a) have red identification
    (b) be accessible only to qualified personnel
    (c) be identified as "FIRE ALARM CIRCUIT"
    (d) all of these

28. Article _____ covers the installation of coaxial cables for distributing radio frequency signals typically employed in community antenna television (CATV) systems.

    (a) 300
    (b) 430
    (c) 800
    (d) 820

29. Antenna discharge units shall be located outside the building only.

    (a) True
    (b) False

30. Raceways enclosing cables and conductors for fire alarm systems must be large enough to permit the _____ of conductors without damaging conductor insulation as limited by 300.17.

    (a) installation
    (b) removal
    (c) splicing
    (d) a and b

31. Audio system circuits using Class 2 or Class 3 wiring methods are not permitted in the same cable, raceway, or cable routing assembly with _____.

    (a) other audio system circuits
    (b) Class 2 conductors or cables
    (c) Class 3 conductors or cables
    (d) b or c

32. Since Class 3 control circuits permit higher allowable levels of voltage and current than Class 2 control circuits, additional _____ are specified to provide protection against the electric shock hazard.

    (a) circuits
    (b) safeguards
    (c) conditions
    (d) requirements

33. In installations where the communications cable enters a building, the metallic sheath members of the cable shall be _____ as close as practicable to the point of entrance.

    (a) grounded as specified in 800.100
    (b) interrupted by an insulating joint or equivalent device
    (c) a or b
    (d) a and b

34. Exposed CATV cables shall be secured by hardware such as straps, staples, cable ties, hangers, or similar fittings designed and installed so as not to damage the cables.

    (a) True
    (b) False

35. Communications cables not terminated at both ends with a connector or other equipment and not identified for future use with a tag are considered abandoned.

    (a) True
    (b) False

36. Outdoor antennas and lead-in conductors shall be securely supported and the lead-in conductors shall be securely attached to the antenna, but they shall not be attached to the electric service mast.

    (a) True
    (b) False

37. Access to electrical equipment shall not be denied by an accumulation of CATV coaxial cables that _____ removal of suspended-ceiling panels.

    (a) prevents
    (b) hinders
    (c) blocks
    (d) require

38. Accessible portions of abandoned communications cable shall be removed.

    (a) True
    (b) False

39. The grounding conductor for an antenna mast or antenna discharge unit, if copper, shall not be smaller than 10 AWG.

    (a) True
    (b) False

40. Openings around penetrations of optical fiber cables and communications raceways through fire-resistant–rated walls, partitions, floors, or ceilings shall be _____ using approved methods to maintain the fire-resistance rating.

    (a) closed
    (b) opened
    (c) draft stopped
    (d) firestopped

41. CATV coaxial cables installed _____ on the surface of ceilings and walls shall be supported by the building structure in such a manner that the cables will not be damaged by normal building use.

    (a) exposed
    (b) concealed
    (c) hidden
    (d) a and b

42. Power-supply conductors and Class 1 circuit conductors can occupy the same cable, enclosure, or raceway _____.

    (a) only where both are functionally associated with the equipment powered
    (b) where the circuits involved are not a mixture of ac and dc
    (c) under no circumstances
    (d) none of these

43. Indoor antenna and lead-in conductors for radio and television receiving equipment shall be separated by at least _____ from conductors of any electric light, power, or Class 1 circuit conductors, unless otherwise permitted.

    (a) 2 in.
    (b) 12 in.
    (c) 18 in.
    (d) 6 ft

44. Class 1, 2, and 3 circuits installed through fire-resistant-rated walls, partitions, floors, or ceilings must be firestopped to limit the possible spread of fire or products of combustion.

    (a) True
    (b) False

45. Exposed Class 2 and Class 3 cables shall be supported by straps, staples, hangers, or similar fittings designed and installed so as not to damage the cable.

    (a) True
    (b) False

46. Coaxial cables used for CATV systems shall not be strapped, taped, or attached by any means to the exterior of any _____ as a means of support.

    (a) conduit
    (b) raceway
    (c) raceway-type mast intended for overhead spans of such cables
    (d) a or b

47. Conductive optical fiber cables contain noncurrent-carrying conductive members such as metallic _____.

    (a) strength members
    (b) vapor barriers
    (c) armor or sheath
    (d) any of these

48. Openings around penetrations of communications cables, communications raceways, and cable routing assemblies through fire-resistant–rated walls, partitions, floors, or ceilings shall be _____ using approved methods to maintain the fire-resistance rating.

    (a) closed
    (b) opened
    (c) draft stopped
    (d) firestopped

49. Fire alarm cables that are not terminated at equipment and not identified for future use with a tag are considered abandoned.

    (a) True
    (b) False

50. Nonconductive optical fiber cable is a factory assembly of one or more optical fibers with an overall covering and containing no electrically conductive materials.

    (a) True
    (b) False

51. Communications grounding electrodes must be bonded to the power grounding electrode system at the building or structure served using a minimum _____ AWG copper bonding jumper.

    (a) 10
    (b) 8
    (c) 6
    (d) 4

52. Nonconductive optical fiber cable contains no metallic members and no other _____ materials.

    (a) electrically conductive
    (b) inductive
    (c) synthetic
    (d) insulating

53. Article _____ contains the installation requirements for the wiring of television and radio receiving equipment, such as digital satellite receiving equipment for television signals and amateur/citizen band radio equipment antennas.

    (a) 680
    (b) 700
    (c) 810
    (d) 840

54. In one- and two-family dwellings where it is not practicable to achieve an overall maximum bonding conductor or equipment grounding conductor length of _____ for CATV, a separate grounding electrode as specified in 250.52(A)(5), (A)(6), or (A)(7) shall be used.

    (a) 5 ft
    (b) 8 ft
    (c) 10 ft
    (d) 20 ft

55. If a separate grounding electrode is installed for the radio and television equipment, it shall be bonded to the building's electrical power grounding electrode system with a bonding jumper not smaller than _____ AWG.

    (a) 10
    (b) 8
    (c) 6
    (d) 1/0

56. Limiting the length of the primary protector grounding conductors for community antenna television and radio systems reduces voltages that may develop between the building's _____ and communications systems during lightning events.

    (a) power
    (b) fire alarm
    (c) lighting
    (d) lightning protection

57. Equipment supplying Class 2 or Class 3 circuits shall be durably marked where plainly visible to indicate _____.

    (a) each circuit that is a Class 2 or Class 3 circuit
    (b) the circuit VA rating
    (c) the size of conductors serving each circuit
    (d) all of these

58. The grounding electrode conductor for an antenna mast shall be _____ protected where subject to physical damage.

    (a) electrically
    (b) mechanically
    (c) arc-fault
    (d) none of these

59. When practicable, a separation of at least _____ ft shall be maintained between communications cables on buildings and lightning conductors.

    (a) 6
    (b) 8
    (c) 10
    (d) 12

60. A bonding jumper not smaller than _____ copper or equivalent shall be connected between the CATV system's grounding electrode and the power grounding electrode system at the building or structure served where separate electrodes are used.

    (a) 12 AWG
    (b) 8 AWG
    (c) 6 AWG
    (d) 4 AWG

61. Access to electrical equipment shall not be denied by an accumulation of optical fiber cables that _____ removal of panels, including suspended-ceiling panels.

    (a) prevents
    (b) hinders
    (c) blocks
    (d) require

62. Generally speaking, conductors for lighting or power may occupy the same enclosure or raceway with conductors of power-limited fire alarm circuits.

    (a) True
    (b) False

63. Access to electrical equipment shall not be denied by an accumulation of remote-control, signaling, or power-limited wire and cables that prevent removal of panels, including suspended-ceiling panels.

    (a) True
    (b) False

64. Composite optical fiber cables contain optical fibers and _____.

    (a) strength members
    (b) vapor barriers
    (c) current-carrying electrical conductors
    (d) none of these

65. Conductive optical fiber cables can occupy the same cable tray, raceway, box, enclosure, or cable routing assembly with conductors for electric light, power, and Class 1 circuits.

    (a) True
    (b) False

66. The conductor used to ground the outer cover of a CATV coaxial cable shall be permitted to be _____.

    (a) insulated
    (b) 14 AWG minimum
    (c) bare
    (d) all of these

67. CATV coaxial cable can deliver power to equipment that is directly associated with the radio frequency distribution system if the voltage is not over _____ and if the current supply is from a transformer or other power-limiting device.

    (a) 60V
    (b) 120V
    (c) 180V
    (d) 270V

68. Accessible portions of abandoned Class 2 and Class 3 cables shall be removed.

    (a) True
    (b) False

69. Where communications wires and cables are installed in a Chapter 3 raceway, the raceway shall be installed in accordance with Chapter 3 requirements.

    (a) True
    (b) False

70. If remote-control, signaling, and power-limited circuits are installed in a raceway that is subjected to different temperatures, and where condensation is known to be a problem, the raceway must be filled with a material approved by the authority having jurisdiction that will prevent the circulation of warm air to a colder section of the raceway. An explosionproof seal _____.

    (a) is required for this purpose
    (b) has been proven effective for this purpose
    (c) isn't required for this purpose
    (d) is the only method of doing this

71. Exposed communications cables shall be secured by hardware including straps, staples, cable ties, hangers, or similar fittings designed and installed so as not to damage the cable.

    (a) True
    (b) False

72. Radio and television receiving antenna systems must have bonding or grounding electrode conductors that are _____.

    (a) copper or other corrosion-resistant conductive material
    (b) insulated, covered, or bare
    (c) securely fastened in place and protected where subject to physical damage
    (d) all of these

73. Equipment intended to be permanently electrically connected to a communications network shall be listed.

    (a) True
    (b) False

74. In one- and two-family dwellings, the grounding electrode conductor for CATV shall be as short as practicable, not to exceed _____ in length.

    (a) 5 ft
    (b) 8 ft
    (c) 10 ft
    (d) 20 ft

75. Outside plant communications cables shall not be required to be listed where the length of the cable within the building, measured from its point of entrance, does not exceed _____ ft and the cable enters the building from the outside and is terminated in an enclosure or on a listed primary protector.

    (a) 25
    (b) 30
    (c) 50
    (d) 100

76. CATV cable not terminated at equipment other than a coaxial cable connector and not identified for future use with a tag is considered abandoned.

    (a) True
    (b) False

77. Communications cables installed _____ on the surface of ceilings and walls shall be supported by the building structure in such a manner that the cable will not be damaged by normal building use.

    (a) exposed
    (b) concealed
    (c) hidden
    (d) a and b

78. In one- and two-family dwellings, the primary protector bonding conductor or grounding electrode conductor for communications systems shall be as short as practicable, not to exceed _____ ft in length.

    (a) 5
    (b) 8
    (c) 10
    (d) 20

79. Underground antenna conductors for radio and television receiving equipment shall be separated at least _____ from any light, power, or Class 1 circuit conductors.

    (a) 12 in.
    (b) 18 in.
    (c) 5 ft
    (d) 6 ft

80. Power-limited fire alarm cable used in a _____ location shall be listed for use in _____ locations or have a moisture-impervious metal sheath.

    (a) dry
    (b) damp
    (c) wet
    (d) hazardous

81. Class 2 and Class 3 cable not terminated at equipment and not identified for future use with a tag is considered abandoned.

    (a) True
    (b) False

82. Accessible portions of abandoned CATV cable shall be removed unless tagged for future use.

    (a) True
    (b) False

83. Class 2 cables identified for future use shall be marked with a tag of sufficient durability to withstand _____.

    (a) moisture
    (b) humidity
    (c) the environment involved
    (d) none of these

84. If the building or structure served has an intersystem bonding termination, the bonding conductor for an antenna mast shall be connected to the intersystem bonding termination.

    (a) True
    (b) False

85. Communications circuits are circuits that extend _____ and outside wiring for fire alarms and burglar alarms from the communications utility to the customer's communications equipment up to and including equipment such as a telephone, fax machine, or answering machine.

    (a) voice
    (b) audio and video
    (c) interactive services
    (d) all of these

86. Audio system circuits using Class 2 or Class 3 wiring methods shall not be installed in the same cable, raceway, or cable routing assembly with _____.

    (a) other audio system circuits
    (b) power-limited fire alarm conductors or cables
    (c) a or b
    (d) none of these

87. Community antenna television and radio system coaxial cables shall not be required to be listed and marked where the length of the cable within the building, measured from its point of entrance, does not exceed _____ ft, the cable enters the building from the outside and the cable is terminated at a grounding block.

    (a) 25
    (b) 30
    (c) 50
    (d) 100

88. Exposed optical fiber cables shall be supported by the building structure using hardware including straps, staples, cable ties, hangers, or similar fittings designed and installed so as not to damage the cable.

    (a) True
    (b) False

89. The point of entrance of an optical fiber installation is the point _____ at which the optical fiber cable emerges from an external wall, from a concrete floor slab, from rigid metal conduit, or from intermediate metal conduit.

    (a) outside a building
    (b) within a building
    (c) on the building
    (d) none of these

90. Fire alarm cables identified for future use shall be marked with a tag of sufficient durability to withstand _____.

    (a) moisture
    (b) humidity
    (c) the environment involved
    (d) none of these

91. Exposed fire alarm circuit cables shall be supported by the building structure using straps, staples, hangers, cable ties or similar fittings designed and installed so as not to damage the cable.

    (a) True
    (b) False

92. Communications wires and cables shall be separated by at least 2 in. from conductors of _____ circuits, unless permitted otherwise.

    (a) power
    (b) lighting
    (c) Class 1
    (d) all of these

93. The power source for a power-limited fire alarm circuit can be supplied through a ground-fault circuit interrupter or an arc-fault circuit interrupter.

    (a) True
    (b) False

94. Cable splices or terminations in power-limited fire alarm systems shall be made in listed _____ or utilization equipment.

    (a) fittings
    (b) boxes or enclosures
    (c) fire alarm devices
    (d) any of these

95. The bonding conductor or grounding electrode conductor for an antenna mast or antenna discharge unit shall be run to the grounding electrode in as straight a line as practicable.

    (a) True
    (b) False

96. Coaxial cables can be installed in any Chapter 3 raceway in accordance with the requirements of Chapter 3.

    (a) True
    (b) False

97. For buildings with grounding means but without an intersystem bonding termination, the grounding conductor for communications circuits shall terminate to the nearest _____.

    (a) building or structure grounding electrode system
    (b) interior metal water piping system, within 5 ft from its point of entrance
    (c) service equipment enclosure
    (d) any of these

98. Fire alarm circuits shall be identified at all terminal and junction locations in a manner that helps prevent unintentional signals on fire alarm system circuits during _____ of other systems.

    (a) installation
    (b) testing and servicing
    (c) renovations
    (d) all of these

99. Accessible portions of abandoned fire alarm cable shall be removed.

    (a) True
    (b) False

100. Indoor antenna lead-in conductors for radio and television receiving equipment can be in the same enclosure with conductors of other wiring systems where separated by an effective permanently installed barrier.

    (a) True
    (b) False

INDEX

Notes

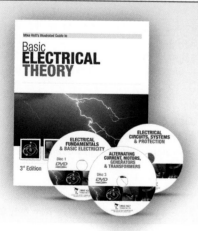

Notes

Mike Holt's Understanding 2014 NEC Requirements for Limited Energy & Communications Systems